The Plays of Aristide Tarnagda

The Plays of Aristide Tarnagda

Contemporary Francophone Theatre from Burkina Faso

Edited by
HEATHER JEANNE DENYER *and* ANNA G. R. MILLER

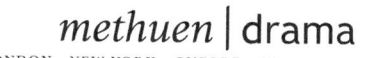

LONDON • NEW YORK • OXFORD • NEW DELHI • SYDNEY

METHUEN DRAMA
Bloomsbury Publishing Plc
50 Bedford Square, London, WC1B 3DP, UK
1385 Broadway, New York, NY 10018, USA
29 Earlsfort Terrace, Dublin 2, Ireland

BLOOMSBURY, METHUEN DRAMA and the Methuen Drama logo are trademarks of
Bloomsbury Publishing Plc

First published in Great Britain 2025

Copyright © Aristide Tarnagda, 2025
Translation © Heather Jeanne Denyer and Anna G. R. Miller, 2025

Aristide Tarnagda, Heather Jeanne Denyer and Anna G. R. Miller have asserted their rights under the Copyright, Designs and Patents Act, 1988, to be identified as author and editors of this work.

Cover design: Matt Thame
Cover image: Sophie Garcia

All rights reserved. No part of this publication may be reproduced or transmitted in any form or by any means, electronic or mechanical, including photocopying, recording, or any information storage or retrieval system, without prior permission in writing from the publishers.

Bloomsbury Publishing Plc does not have any control over, or responsibility for, any third-party websites referred to or in this book. All internet addresses given in this book were correct at the time of going to press. The author and publisher regret any inconvenience caused if addresses have changed or sites have ceased to exist, but can accept no responsibility for any such changes.

No rights in incidental music or songs contained in the work are hereby granted and performance rights for any performance/presentation whatsoever must be obtained from the respective copyright owners.

All rights whatsoever in this play are strictly reserved and application for performance etc. should be made before rehearsals to Permissions Department, Bloomsbury Publishing Plc, 50 Bedford Square, London, WC1B 3DP, UK. No performance may be given unless a licence has been obtained. No rights in incidental music or songs contained in the Work are hereby granted and performance rights for any performance/presentation whatsoever must be obtained from the respective copyright owners.

A catalogue record for this book is available from the British Library.

A catalog record for this book is available from the Library of Congress.

ISBN: HB: 978-1-3504-5313-5
PB: 978-1-3504-5306-7
ePDF: 978-1-3504-5315-9
eBook: 978-1-3504-5314-2

Series: Methuen Drama Play Collections

Typeset by RefineCatch Limited, Bungay, Suffolk
Printed and bound in Great Britain

To find out more about our authors and books visit www.bloomsbury.com and sign up for our newsletters.

Contents

List of Figures vi
Introduction 1

And If I Killed Them All, Ma'am? 9
Tears from the August Sky 33
Red Earth 59
Ways of Loving 81
Sank, or the Patience of the Dead 105
Musika 137

Afterword 163
List of Contributors 166

Figures

1. Hamidou Bonssa, Lamine Diarra, David Malgoubri, and Salif Ouedraogo in *Et si je les tuais tous madame?* (*And If I Killed Them All, Ma'am?*), directed by Aristide Tarnagda in 2012 at the Récréâtrales Festival in Ouagadougou, Burkina Faso. Photo © Emile Zeizig   11
2. Ramatou Ouedraogo in *Les larmes du ciel d'août* (*Tears from the August Sky*), directed by Aristide Tarnagda in 2023 for the FARaway Festival at the Comédie de Reims in France. Photo © Vincent VDH   35
3. Kiswend-sida Urbain Guiguemdé in *Terre rouge* (*Red Earth*), directed by Miriam Lustig in 2021 at Theater Stok in Zürich, Switzerland. Photo © Christina Steybe   62
4. Lionelle Edoxi Gnoula and Safourata Kaboré in *Façons d'aimer* (*Ways of Loving*), directed by Aristide Tarnagda in 2015 at the Festival les Francophonies in Limoges, France. Photo © Christophe Péan   84
5. David Malgoubri, Alain Hema, and Alberto Martinez Guinaldo in *Sank, ou la patience des morts* (*Sank, or the Patience of the Dead*), codirected by Aristide Tarnagda and Pierre Lambotte in 2016 at the Théâtre de la Guimbarde (Belgium) in collaboration with the Théâtre Eclair (Burkina Faso). Photo © Valérie Burton   109
6. Nadège Ouedraogo in *Musika*, directed by Odile Sankara in 2018 at the Récréâtrales Festival in Ouagadougou, Burkina Faso. Photo © Heather Jeanne Denyer   141

Introduction

Heather Jeanne Denyer

Aristide Tarnagda, Burkinabè Theatre Artist

This book gathers six plays by Aristide Tarnagda to share with a wider readership, particularly one that reads English. The politically charged and poetically rendered theatre of this award-winning playwright is an essential edition to studies in global literature and world theatre of the twenty-first century because it speaks with naked honesty, like many of the characters, from the red dust of Burkina Faso to a global humanity. In a world grappling with wars, famine, climate change, and other ramifications of colonialism and neocolonization, we turn to the arts for a sense of meaning. Tarnagda contends that "challenges are important for us, artists, because in moments of uncertainty, of panic, of losing peace, the artists are the ones who can work to return calm, joy, happiness, and above all, clarity" (Denyer 2020, 7).

After starting out as an actor in 1999, then working as a director, he tried his hand at writing for the stage in a 2004 workshop led by Ivorian playwright Koffi Kwahulé. There, he found his talent for giving voice to marginalized Africans. Beginning with his earlier plays: *Et si je les tuais tous madame?* (*And If I Killed Them All, Ma'am?*) and *Les larmes du ciel d'août* (*Tears from the August Sky*), both published in French in 2013, Tarnagda began making a name for himself as an up-and-coming writer of prowess in Francophone theatre scenes, including the festival of Francophone theatre in Limoges and the renowned Avignon Festival.

The following two plays, *Terre Rouge* (*Red Earth*) and *Façons d'aimer* (*Ways of Loving*), published together, won Tarnagda the prestigious Grand Prix de littéraire d'Afrique noire (Best African Literary Work), awarded by the French-Language Writers' Association in 2017. Along with the two earlier plays, they are presented as long monologues, directly focusing on the need for the speakers' voices to be heard. Each character speaks with keen urgency at a pivotal moment in their life, and each does so through an irresistible lyricism and palpable passion. Tarnagda concedes: "I've always anchored my characters in dire situations where they have to make tough choices, where they have to define themselves and take charge of their own fate. They can't be indifferent" (Tarnagda 2018, 6). While we may turn away from news of fighting in Sudan or of migrants dying in Libya, these compelling plays force audiences and readers to not remain indifferent to their plights.

In the last two plays of this collection, *Sank, ou la patience des morts* (*Sank, or the Patience of the Dead*) (2016) and *Musika* (2019), the playwright tackles pressing social and political problems even more directly and with larger casts. His aim becomes clear in these works, as he notes: "I always like to blend the intimate and the political. Because the intimate allows an opening up" (Tarnagda 2018, 5). Yet, even with a sharper sense of political urgency, there are moments of penetrating rhythm and glimpses of sharp imagery—not to mention the pervasive humor—that compel readers and audiences to relate to the characters who find themselves trapped in the darkest mine of the Congo forest or fighting in the darkest hours of revolutionary violence.

These plays illustrate Tarnagda's efforts to "transcend reality" through his theatre, as he explained in our 2018 interview: "It's in speaking about our realities that we can transcend them" (Tarnagda 2018, 5). The realities reflected through these plays resonate not only in his home of Burkina Faso, but in other parts of Africa, and they implicate all audiences, including those of us reading from the US, the UK, Canada, and Europe.

Burkina Faso became independent from France in 1962. The country, formerly known as Upper Volta, was renamed by Thomas Sankara in 1984 as the land of the upright people. As desertification of the country increases, so do attacks by groups affiliated with Al Qaeda, ISIL, and other terrorist groups, and a great part of the country lacks access to basic resources. Between 2019 and 2021 alone, nearly 1.4 million people were displaced. People struggle with diseases, risks of famine, and violence, as in many other parts of the world today. Burkina Faso has experienced four coup d'états in the twenty-first century thus far, including two in 2022, at which time the constitution was suspended and the French military, journalists, and the ambassador left. These are harsh realities, indeed.

Burkinabè cultural life, however, and particularly theatre there demonstrates the resilience of the people to transcend these realities. The country has been a hub for West African theatre since 1992 when the late director, Jean-Pierre Guingané, founded the Festival International de Théâtre et de Marionnettes (International Festival of Theatre and Puppets of Ouagadougou, or FITMO) and his theatre company, Théâtre de la Fraternité (the Brotherhood Theatre), where Tarnagda began as an actor.

Now directed by Tarnagda himself, the Récréâtrales Festival draws over 3,000 audience members to attend performances every day during its biennial week-long festival. Founded in 2002 to encompass both residences and resistance efforts, the festival brings together African artists not only from Burkina Faso, but from Cameroon, the Congo, Guinea, Rwanda, and many other countries to participate in development workshops while lodging at local homes in the Bougsemtenga working-class neighborhood in the capital, Ouagadougou. Young artists train in acting, directing, and design, and playwrights develop new works that are then fully brought to life during the festival. A few play highlights from Les Récréâtrales in recent years include Guinean Hakim Bah's *Gentil petit chien* (*Dear Little Dog*), which tackles the aftermath of the 2015 Paris terrorist attack, *Une plaidoirie pour vendre le Congo* (*A Plea to Sell the Congo*) by playwright Sinzo Aanza of the Democratic Republic of the Congo, and Dieudonné Niangouna—a well-established playwright from the Republic of the Congo—directing his own adaptation of Shakespeare's *The Tempest* via Aimé Césaire's *A Tempest: Prospero*, a new colonization play set on Mars. Other Burkinabé artists have developed as theatre makers and presented works as part of the festival, including actress Safourata Kaboré and actress-writer Lionelle Edoxi Gnoula, who co-wrote the preface to *Ways of Loving* in this collection, and writer-director-performer Odile Sankara, who wrote the preface for *Musika*. Etienne Minoungou, himself an accomplished writer, director, and performer, was the first director of Les Récréâtrales; he has written the afterword for this volume.

Tarnagda's work was first presented in the US in 2018 in a reading of my translation of *Ways of Loving* as part of PEN World Voices Festival. During our time together at the Martin E. Segal Theatre Center in New York, I interviewed Tarnagda for the website Howlround.com, and something he said continues to resonate with me as important for non-African readers and audiences to understand. He clarified that he is a playwright—a Burkinabè playwright, yes, but also a playwright, simply put, because he writes for everyone. In the local performances at Les Récréâtrales, he and his colleagues bring theatre to the people and use theatre to create community. He explains: "In order to promote people coming together, it's essential that theatre is about them, that it interests them and speaks to them" (Tarnagda 2018, 5). So, his theatre is about local audiences in his home country, and it is also about all Africans. And those of us in the Global North, we, too, are implicated in these plays.

The reality of how interconnected we really are, even while separated geographically, can be appreciated in great moments of theatre performance shared by transnational audiences. It can also be recognized in our experiences during the Covid-19 pandemic. In the April 10, 2020, "Covid-Time Segal Theatre Talks" interview between Tarnagda and Martin E. Segal Theatre Center Director Frank Hentschker streamed on Howlround. com, the playwright made a pertinent observation: thousands die in his country every year from malaria and no one seems to notice; but when thousands in the Global North are dying from a disease, everyone takes notice. He explained: "What I see here on a daily basis is that the fear that people feel of dying is more about starvation than dying from this disease.

4 The Plays of Aristide Tarnagda

Because if they cannot go outside to seek their daily bread, even if they don't have coronavirus, they will die of hunger" (Denyer 2020, 7). When we consider how Tarnagda's theatre works to transcend realities, we can truly appreciate how he is at once writing specifically to engage fellow Burkinabé citizens, while also writing for all of us, for all of humanity. Reading his plays brings us a little bit closer together in this way.

A Project of Transcultural Translation

This publication is an effort towards bridging boundaries through theatre that transcend linguistic, cultural, and geographic borders to open broader discussions. It is a small step towards representing African literature in world literature and African theatre in world theatre, and towards recognizing some of the incredible heretofore neglected talent in both areas. With these plays, we invite readers in English-speaking parts of the world including the US and Canada, the UK and Australia, as well as in Africa to connect with these plays. As you will find with each work, those of us reading from the Global North are part of the worlds of these plays, even when they are set in Africa; even when the characters relate cultural or political realities different from our own.

As editors and translators of this volume, Anna Miller and I both experienced the power of Tarnagda's theatre through performance. My first exposure was in Limoges for the 2015 premiere production of *Ways of Loving* directed by the playwright, and with the incredible talents of Safourata Kaboré (Daughter) and Lionelle Edoxi Gnoula (Mother). David Malgoubri accompanied them with guitar and offered a voice for the father's and husband's lines. The audience sat, transfixed, as the women shared their stories, which were at once deeply personal, and at the same time, resonant to me as a US-born woman. After attending the 2018 reading of the play translated in New York, Miller proposed the idea of a volume of Tarnagda's plays in translation. Both of us were eager to increase awareness of his powerful, poetic theatre. While *Ways of Loving* is the only translation to have been given voice in the US, *Musika* (2019) was the first published in English translation (published in *PAJ* 41, no. 3, 103–19). Both of these garnered some attention in New York, and my translation of *Musika* is now being taught to US undergraduate students. Nevertheless, a playwright of this stature deserves greater representation in English-language contexts, and we were committed to providing that.

In preparing these translations, Miller, a French scholar, and I, a theatre scholar, were keenly aware of the act of translating not only across languages, but across cultures. As two US American women of European descent whose first language is English translating the words of an African playwright from French, we need to acknowledge our own positionalities. Playwright Véronique Tadjo of Ivory Coast notes that translation is "not only about crossing from one language to another, but it is also about understanding other cultures, entering other world views through empathy" (Tadjo and Batchelor 2013, 100). We can never fully understand the lived experiences and cultural histories of the writers whose work we invest in. Instead, we have developed a relationship with the playwright that is founded in mutual respect and trust. We have done our best to honor his intentions in how the text is presented. To this end, we have included relatively few notes, choosing to not explain every cultural reference. This means that some references will be recognizable for African readers, but not for others. This also includes the choice of not translating the original Bissa text in *Red Earth*, but leaving it intact in recognition of the playwright's first language.

Translating plays is a form of dramaturgy, for the translator as a dramaturg is keenly aware of the storytelling with every syllable, every letter, and every image captured and conferred from one language to another. Translating plays is a multifaceted project as we not only see the words written but hear them being spoken as they will be when staged. In addition to ensuring that meanings in the phrases are clear, we must consider the characters' voices and, at the same time, how to convey to future performers the resonance of each voice. Further, we must bear in mind the possible embodiment of the movement and action in the play. In the case of Tarnagda's theatre, there are few stage directions to indicate the staging of the bodies; still, the musicality of the language often steers a sense of movement. His plays offer levity and poetry through the voices, even while the themes are heavy. We translated them with an eye to their specific cultural contexts, while appreciating that they speak of humanity rather than presenting facile impressions of the African characters and their realities.

For Tarnagda and other African playwrights writing in French, the language changes from what it might be in Europe; it resonates as more sonorous. In Africa, stories were traditionally shared orally and have been alienated to an extent from their African sources when they were written in European forms and languagesguage. Whereas the notion of theatre in the European sense remains largely attached to the written play, theatre forms existed in Africa before being developed in Europe, and the resonances of the origins from storytelling and music remain largely visible in contemporary African theatre. Fellow translator of African theatre from French to English, Marjolijn de Jager likens the language to music, suggesting that a translator must be able to hear when reading, particularly as the nature of African theatre texts is intricately connected to oral traditions involving music (De Jager 2013, 112). In the process of "hearing" the plays in the act of translation, their oral nature is recaptured—as it will be by performers on the stage. Thus, the translation of these contemporary plays invokes an essence of traditional expression in the work.

Translating is, therefore, a way of building bridges between cultures as much as between languages. Tadjo emphasizes the dire need for translation in the global world of today, which we are heeding: "Writing and translation can play a very positive role in promoting peace and cooperation" (Tadjo and Batchelor 2013, 100). Scholars and audiences should increasingly turn to translation as a way of learning from theatres of the Global South to build these bridges to peace.

Let these translated plays take you to the top of the Boulgou, into the Congolese forests, and across the red earth. And when you are there, may the stories remind you of how close we all are as humans in this one world—one community. This is the playwright's goal in his theatre: "We create a community, and, above all, we create connections between people" (Tarnagda 2018, 5). That community is then expanded upon through translating plays. Indeed, translating is activism, as De Jager explains, it "function[s] as a megaphone amplifying the author's words to a larger reading audience" (De Jager 2013, 114). For our part, we hope that you will find in these translated plays the beauty, pain, and the compassion we see, and that someday soon, Tarnagda's theatre will be presented on stages beyond West Africa and Western Europe, that his plays will be read by students and scholars the world over.

We are deeply appreciative to Emile Lansman who published the plays in the original French for the permissions for these translations, to Bonnie Marranca at *PAJ* for permission to republish the translation of *Musika* and to Frank Hentschker for his part in introducing Tarnagda to US audiences. We are indebted to the talented Burkinabé writers of the prefaces and the afterword for contributing to a fuller presentation of theatre in their country today. Most of all, we are profoundly grateful to the playwright for supporting this project and allowing us to play a part in sharing his incredible theatre.

Bibliography

De Jager, Marjolin (2013). "Translation—A Listening Art." In Véronique Tadjo and Kathryn Batchelor (eds.), *Intimate Enemies: Translation in Francophone Contexts*, 109–16. Liverpool: Liverpool University Press.

Denyer, Heather (2020). "Aristide Tarnagda, director and playwright." In Benjamin Gillespie, Sarah Lucie, and Jennifer Joan Thompson (eds.), "Global Voices in the Time of Coronavirus," *PAJ: Performing Arts Journal*, 42 (3): 3–27. Project MUSE.

Tadjo, Véronique and Kathryn Batchelor (2013). "Translation: Spreading the Wings of Literature." In Véronique Tadjo and Kathryn Batchelor (eds.), *Intimate Enemies: Translation in Francophone Contexts*, 98–108. Liverpool: Liverpool University Press.

Tarnagda, Aristide (2018). "Aristide Tarnagda and Theatre in Burkina Faso." Interview by Heather Jeanne Denyer. *Howlround*. November 5. Available online: https://howlround.com/aristide tarnagda-and-theatre-burkina-faso-Aristide-Tarnagda-et-le-theatre-au-burkina-faso.

And If I Killed Them All, Ma'am?

Preface to *And If I Killed Them All, Ma'am?*

By Aristide Tarnagda. Adapted from an interview with the playwright conducted in 2014 by the journalist Anne Bocandé for *Africiné*, the African Federation of Film Critics online magazine based in Dakar, Senegal. Translated by Anna G. R. Miller.

And If I Killed Them All, Ma'am? is a response to an earlier text, *Tears from the August Sky*, in which a young woman in the street refuses a rich woman's offer to get into her car. The young woman says she's waiting for her man. She says she's given up everything to do so. This woman says she's not down on her luck. It's tied to the discourse on the West and Africa where there's this narrative that people are all down on their luck and struggling. Even though they haven't sorted out their own lives, they allow themselves to say to others: "We are going to help you."

I met Lamine Diarra in Avignon at the reading. Something happened between us and I decided that I wanted to work with him. Lamine is from Mali and he had moved to Angers with his family. We talked a lot about his heartache and the place he was struggling to make for himself in France. That's when I said to myself: What if Lamine was the man in *Tears from the August Sky*, the one who leaves to find money "elsewhere," who the woman is waiting for! My initial sense of the play that became *And If I Killed Them All, Ma'am?* appeared to me in this way. I put the characters in the same situations, the same context.

1 Hamidou Bonssa, Lamine Diarra, David Malgoubri, and Salif Ouedraogo in *Et si je les tuais tous madame?* (*And If I Killed Them All, Ma'am?*), directed by Aristide Tarnagda in 2012 at the Récréâtrales Festival in Ouagadougou, Burkina Faso. Photo © Emile Zeizig.

And If I Killed Them All, Ma'am?

Translated by Anna G. R. Miller

And If I Killed Them All, Ma'am? is a play written in monologue form that portrays a man (Lamine) who stands at an intersection far from his home and addresses an unseen, silent woman in her car waiting for the light to turn green. Tarnagda expands the duration of the red light to nearly an hour in productions and fills it with a blend of voices from Lamine's past (the pregnant girlfriend he left behind, his deceased best friend, his mother, and his father), his attempts to explain why he is at this intersection and talking at such length, and his increasing awareness of the wealth imbalance between himself and the driver that ultimately leads to violence. The first version of the play was written in Quebec at the Centre des Auteurs Dramatiques (CEAD) in 2011. It premiered the following year at the Récréâtrales Festival in Ouagadougou, Burkina Faso, and then traveled to the Avignon Theatre Festival in 2013. Among other productions, the play was performed in 2015 at the Théâtre de Poche in Brussels, Belgium, and in France at the Comédie Saint-Etienne (2017) and as part of the FARaway Festival at the Comédie de Reims (2023). The original French version (*Et si je les tuais tous madame?*) was published by Lansman Editeurs in 2013. It has five characters: three men and two women.

Notes on the Translation: The original French edition includes a footnote after Lamine first refers to the *Donzos* explaining that the Donzos are tribes and communities of hunters in West Africa that have a notable presence in Mali. The dedications in italics were written by the playwright. Punctuation and capitalization have only been changed when deemed necessary for comprehension.

Characters

Lamine
His girlfriend
His father
His mother
Robert

To my father
To my mother
To Mandela Tarnagda
And Lamine Diarra

> "It must be terrible to die in a foreign country. It's like you never lived. Because a stranger, he's someone who hangs up his life like you hang up a coat by the front door. He's someone who's waiting to live. . ."
>
> *Crazy Village, or the Screw-Ups* by Koffi Kwahulé

> "I am no great hero, and I too shout, and no one responds. People say the sun brings the universe back to life. The sun will rise and—look at it, is it not a corpse? Everything is dead—corpses everywhere."
>
> *A Gentle Creature* by Fyodor Dostoevsky

A street. A traffic light. The light is red. Light traffic. Some city noises. Lamine has a bag on his back. A woman driving her car waits for the green light.

Lamine Do you know about the Donzos, ma'am?

No?

Yes, ma'am, I know you don't have time, me neither, I don't have it either, that's why I didn't start off with niceties, sorry about that, ma'am, but do you get it? It's this shitty time that means we're always running out of time, so when you stopped, and I came over and you lowered your window, and you said with this deadly and suspicious smile: "yeees!!"

I said to myself: "don't bother embellishing, Lamine, hurry quickly like you did that night not asking yourself if the horizon was blue, if the tide was low or high, if the stars would follow you as you walked, if where you're going it's raining, snowing, sunny, or stormy; if it's true that even after a hundred years of sitting in water a piece of wood never turns into an alligator, that a bird ends up landing whatever his path may be; if it's true that natives know to walk around the hole that the stranger falls into . . ." I said to myself: "hurry, don't look ahead or behind you, hurry kid, hurry for the kid, leave this rat hole of a country and hurry, hurry, don't weigh your options, hurry anywhere, hurry for the kid . . ."

Do you get it, ma'am? Don't get mad at me if I didn't reciprocate your smile, your availability, like a well-educated man would have done, I'll be polite and greet you properly after I tell you about my blood in her belly, about how, one night, every night, when the stars were all laughing, I planted my seed in her belly like you plant a seed in the ground, I forgot myself in her belly and right away her belly began to swell swell swell . . .

Do you know about the Donzos, ma'am? Say something, ma'am, because a red light lasts no more than a minute . . .

Lamine!

You again?

Dammit! Can't you wait just a second? Don't you see the lady doesn't have time? She's already nice enough to listen to me for the length of a red light . . . there aren't tons of people like her here, that's for sure. It's been days, weeks, months since I've been standing here, at this same spot, next to the same light, just waiting to ask for an opinion, a piece of advice, just to know what they would have done if they were in my shoes. Nobody's given me a single second out of the billion seconds I've been here, nobody. Some yelled at me like I was a worthless piece of shit. Others looked at me with pity in their eyes and did nothing. The most cynical ones offered me pennies . . . People are crazy! The moment you go up to them, they think you want cash . . .

Excuse me, ma'am, it's her, she won't stop bothering me, she's been like that for a while, always the same questions, the same complaints:

When are you coming back?

Did you get the money?

Did you forget me?

And him?

The one you stuck in my belly before you left?

What do I do with him?

What do I say to him when he only knows how to say daddy where's daddy, I want my daddy, I want to see my daddy, I want to hug my daddy, I want to dance with my daddy, I want to laugh with my daddy, I want to ride bikes with my daddy, I want to sing with my daddy, I want my daddy to bring me to school, I want my daddy to buy me a treat, I want my daddy's hand, where's my daddy, mommy?

What do I tell him, huh? That he doesn't have a daddy? That his daddy's a dog who pissed him into his mommy's hole and disappeared into thin air, off to another shitty part of the world, off to look for other bitches to piss in their holes and add more dogs to this world? What do I tell this puppy you stuck in my belly who won't stop barking daddy daddy daddy?! Do I tell him he's better off without a daddy because his own daddy's a man who says nothing? Who's a worthless piece of shit?

Did you hear, ma'am? I'm a worthless piece of shit, it's like that every day, every night, for days now, weeks, months, it's like that in my head, so tell me what I should do, tell me what you would have done if you were in my shoes, I know nobody can put themselves in another person's shoes, but what can you do, there's no space left anywhere and we've got to put ourselves somewhere, so tell me something, quickly ma'am, the light's going to turn green, and everyone's going to start honking like crazy, people don't know how to wait anymore, they don't have time to wait anymore, they want to run run run to what? To where? God only knows; some say to work, some say home, when everyone's looking for work, everyone's looking for a place to stay, all while birds glide across the sky laughing at us for not knowing how to rise above the nightmares and laugh at our dreams, all while dogs run through the streets and flirt with bitches and don't give a shit about work, about home, all while their puppies play in the sun scratching off each other's fleas, all while we, in our little corners, ignore each other and drink our Cokes, our beers, all while investments grow and we find more and more holes in our pockets and termites chew away at Karl Marx's bones, tell me something, ma'am, tell me if you know about the Donzos, just tell me if I should leave again or stay . . .

Yes, ma'am, I'm not from here, I don't know if I'm really from somewhere, if I'll be from somewhere someday, maybe if you tell me what I should do, I'll find myself a somewhere . . .

Of course, ma'am, I've got parents, everyone does, but things went downhill fast with them . . .

My dad?

We got into it early on, me and my dad, when I was ten . . .

Because of my friend, my friend Robert, it was our neighbors across the street, my dad didn't want anyone to go to Robert's house, he said Robert and I, we weren't a good match as friends . . .

Why?

Robert didn't go to school . . .

Why didn't Robert go to school?

Because Robert's parents couldn't afford Robert's tuition, but Robert didn't give a shit, Robert didn't get bored shitless like we got bored shitless at school rehashing the same stuff over and over again like idiots, seeing the same faces every day of the year, sitting in the same seats every day of the year, no ma'am, Robert had fun, he had fun and he made things, Robert was an artist, at ten, I'm not making this up, ma'am, ten-year-old Robert was an extremely gifted artist, he wandered around all day, he picked up empty cans, milk containers, Robert went dumpster diving, he picked up the Budweiser-Heineken-Coors-Guinness-Mountain Dew bottles, the Coke-Pepsi cans, the Yamaha-Honda bike ignition coils that mechanics threw out, Robert wandered around in town like the stars wander around in the sky; and with Budweiser-Coke-Heineken-Coors-Mountain Dew-Yamaha-Pepsi-Honda-Guinness, Robert made airplanes, helicopters, motorcycles, trailers, trains, boats, I swear it's true, ma'am, I saw Robert make all of that, I even made some of it with him, it's true, ma'am, I'll explain quickly, because soon the red light will be gone and you'll need to leave, but you have to help me choose before you go, will you help me ma'am? Thank you so much, if you help me, I'll make you a plane, a Robert plane, a plane that can land anywhere . . .

Yes, ma'am, Robert's planes can land anywhere, even in water . . .

What are you telling this woman, Lamine?

Robert?

Hurry up

The red light's fading

Her too

Him too

Steal the lady's bag

No, Robert

Yes, Lamine

No, Robert

Yes, Lamine

No, Robert

Don't do something stupid, Lamine

No, Robert

The fucking bag!

The bag Lamine! There's tons of money in the bag. Tons of cash. She's going to stick it in the bank, the bank, Lamine, what a joke; that's what you used to say, the bank's a joke, people stick their pennies in the bank when we need them . . . she's got a million dollars in her bag, she's going to stick it in the bank . . .

No, Robert

Yes, Lamine

Don't mess around, the wallet's in the bag, the Louis Vuitton wallet, inside Louis Vuitton there's the credit cards, in those cards there are millions and millions . . .

Shut up Robert, shut up Robert, shut up Robert . . .

You're the one who's going to fuck this up, what are you thinking? That she'll say: "poor young man listen I think you need to go back and take care of your sweetheart and your kid . . ." You think she's going to calmly open her wallet and tell you: "take this, get a plane, a bus, I don't know, but hurry back home, enroll your kid in school, take care of his mother, find yourself a job instead of wandering around here like Robert"?

Robert

Shit, Lamine. She doesn't give a fucking shit, Walaï, I swear to God, she doesn't care . . .

That flowers are withering

That oases of water are disappearing from the desert

That murderers' bullets are turning doves red

What do you think, Lamine? That the Muslim would get anywhere near undercooked dog meat or anything haram?

Do you hear yourself talking, Robert, do you at least, no seriously, do you hear yourself, Robert? What happened, Robert? What happened goddammit that got you this stuck in the mud?

Lamine, I was always in the mud

It's not true, you were an artist

An artist in the mud, my man

Artists are people in the mud

You'd say you transformed things, that you gave them new life, new meaning, I reinvented things, you'd say . . .

We're here to talk about the girl who doesn't know what to do anymore, not me! Who's waiting for you, who's waiting for you, who's waiting for you because you told her to wait for you there. She said: "you don't need to go, my love" and you said to her: "I have to go because our son's coming soon and he needs money, wait for me here, I'll come back here and find you, you and our son, with our son's money . . ." And she took a blood oath, she drank of her own blood to say that she'll never never never move and you took a blood oath, you drank of your own blood to say that . . .

Shut up, Robert

That you'll come back

Shut up

With your son's money

Shut up, Robert

And you abandoned her in the middle of the road with a switchblade and nothing else

Screw you, Robert

Why a switchblade for a girl whose belly you filled up with your blood, at night, every night, with the stars as your witnesses, with the smell of rotten meat, rotten mango, piss, mosquitos, cardboard sheets

Because you know how it is over there

You're lying, Lamine. You're lying to yourself, and that's not good for your health. You can lie to other people and not get sick, but lying to yourself means you don't give a shit if the cancer spreads from your stomach to your belly my friend; you freaked out when you saw you were filling her belly you were petrified my friend and you told yourself: "what do I do how do I feed the kid how where do I house the kid how do I take care of the kid," you freaked out my friend and you told yourself: "I'm getting out of here, she'll figure it out on her own I'll find myself a calm sunny place where I won't see when flies swarm around her wounds I'll hide somewhere church bells will muffle her cries."

It's not true, ma'am, don't listen to him, Robert's bullshitting, I'll explain it to you, when she started gaining weight and suddenly puking, when she told me:

My period

What about your period?

It's been two months since I got my period

It started like that, ma'am

Suddenly like that

Like an August rain

An August rain that, like an eraser, erases the houses made of straw and mud. The cardboard houses. The tar. An August rain that erases everything and plants in us the fear of mosquitos and malaria. When there's no vaccine yet for malaria, for malaria that kills thousands of women and children each day. When the government only talks about emergence, development, positive growth, newly discovered gold mines, the president's trips to see other heads of state . . . August delivers us mosquitos and Chinese people who come to sell us phones. Motorcycles. Bridges. Stadiums to play soccer under the burning August sun and sweat out the malaria. For the Americans, it's the Millennium Challenge.

For the French from the NewFrenchAfrica, it's aid for development and emergence and for that, ma'am, we really have to emerge, because nobody there sees us under the mosquitos planting malaria in our bodies, nobody sees us in our TVs that only talk about Ronaldo, Messi, and Beckham, and about their league of champions and about their first league and about their Bollywood and about their Hollywood and about our president who cries out everywhere he goes that the August sky bites everyone, and that his friends the Great Democracies must help us with water, light, schools, tents, when his personal zoo . . .

It'll be August soon, Lamine

Do you remember, Robert?

Do you remember we were happy in August?

We were always staring up at the sky. We wanted the August sky to fill with black clouds. And every time, as if the sky heard us, it would suddenly start to darken. Suddenly, the sky began to piss. Endlessly. Like a drunk. Quietly, I'd leave our house and come to yours. I'd help you put out buckets and dishes under the roof at your houses to collect the water . . . angels' piss, that's what you'd say, you'd say water from the sky was piss from angels who'd hide and drink when God was worn out and asleep. We'd collect a lot of angel piss for your mom. Then we'd get naked, you and I, we'd get naked in the rain and we'd run we'd run we'd run and we'd run in every direction, we'd laugh, we'd sing, we'd dance in the angel piss, we'd go out onto the roads, we'd gather the dry sand holding out against the angel piss and we'd build houses with the sand that would slip away instantly, do you remember? Do you remember that like idiots we'd throw the sand onto our stomachs, onto our faces? Do you remember, Robert, the sand was beautiful, fine?

I remember the smell of the sand on our lips

I remember our sandy bodies

Do you remember that with our bodies all sandy we'd go to the river banks? Right, Robert? We'd throw ourselves in the rivers, we'd hold our breath in the river, I didn't know how to swim and you'd make me drink the river water and I'd cough, and you'd hold my head underwater, and you'd sing a song the gurgling of the water coming through my nostrils, my mouth, my drunk ears would drown out . . .

Sing

Sing

Sing, Robert

Sing me that clearly beautiful song I never heard in that river full of angel piss.

Sing, Robert

Sing with your voice that I sensed from deep underwater

Remind me of my friend and sing

Sing about the water that like angels would start to piss fish, lots of fish that would fall from the sky with the angel piss, lots of fish to collect when my head came out of the water . . . Do you remember I'd say you should sell the fish so we could buy ourselves cookies? And you'd say you wanted to give the sky fish to your mom. Do you remember, Robert? Do you remember after our heads were out of the water, after we got the sand off our bodies . . . Do you remember those pisses in August that made us so cold we'd shiver? You'd say: "wouldn't it be nice if there were girls here to hold us and make this cold in our bodies disappear . . ." you'd say girls could drink up the cold the angel piss left on us. You were right, my friend, yes you are right, you bastard, and that's what's annoying about you, my friend, you are always right

You know, that's how it started with her, it started with the cold the August sky dumps on our bodies, that bastard of an August sky that mistakes our bodies for dens to house the cold . . . Yes I know you know what it is to have your body turned into a den . . . but you see, you were right . . .

That day, I'd just finished unloading ten tons of cement off the truck, so with two thousand francs in hand, I hurried to the store and lit a cigarette and suddenly the sky that rumbles, wails, storms, well you know how it is when the sky begins to lose it all of a sudden like a corporal trying to lead a coup, it runs, my friend, it honks, and the sudden dust, the dust, the hens, the dogs, the sheep, you've got everything starting to run all of a sudden, and I'm stuck in this sudden race, are you following me, my friend? You've got to follow me, because now it's vertigo. Eyes blinded by the sun and fighting off the dust, lips blowing cigarette smoke in the storm's face, its body willowy, tranquil, motionless in the heart of the market at the doorstep of this sheet metal house that begins to itch all of a sudden, and the girl who laughs about all that, and me caught in her laughter, keep up, my friend, because I can't keep up with her at all, she looks at me, she looks at me, she gives me vertigo, unloads it on me like I unload bags of cement in stores, she gives me actual butterflies in my stomach, you see, my friend? So I stop. I stop there with her, and the silence, and our two cigarettes blowing their smoke in protest against the cold the sky is preparing to release onto our bodies, into our bodies, we smoke, we smoke, we hear only our stillness, the sky laughs at our cigarette smoke and begins to piss, and the cold the cold the cold draws us closer, she gets closer, my man, do you remember the cold from the August sky, Robert? She gets closer, I get closer, do you remember thinking girls could drink up the cold the sky plants in our bodies? She gets closer, I get closer, and then we're one, and then we're naked . . .

It'll be August soon, Lamine

I know, Robert

She and the kid will be underwater. You know how the August sky is, you have to go back, alone she could've figured it out, but with the kid, what can she do with the kid under the August sky?

And if I were dead

You're not dead

She could act as if I were

You aren't

I am

You aren't

I'm telling you I am! What is a man far from his home? Far from his woman's heart, from her body? Far from his kid's laughter, his cries? What is a man without friends to tell him: "don't do this, do that"?

You're the one who wanted to go

What a joke

She said

She said she said she said and me I decided

You promised

I'll keep my promise

So what are you waiting for?

I didn't get the money

The lady's loaded

I don't want to steal the lady's money

Why?

I'd be ashamed to face the kid and her

And you're not ashamed now?

What about now?

Look what she's doing

Look what you're making her do

Look what she's become

A thing

A piece of merchandise

Reified

Objectified

Screwed

Look how she comes and goes every day and night

Washing ironing sweeping cleaning emptying stopping suffering tiring abandoning forgetting

The kid

The kid wakes up in the middle of the night and sings a song. The same monotone song

Fatality

Banality

Obscurity

Delight

Exile

Alone. Mommy alone. Daddy left alone. Without us. In the middle of the night. Before the cock's crow. When the dogs were in heat. While the stars lit our dark faces. Daddy left to bring dreams back to us, mommy said. He's late he's late he's late daddy, daddy, mommy . . .

It's the kid, it's the kid, it's the kid, he's so beautiful! He's like his dad! He's my spitting image! He has some of her in his eyes! His eyes are sky blue, like her, the horizon in his eyes! I'm so proud!

No reason to be, Lamine

Yes there is, Robert

No, Lamine

Yes, Robert

No, Lamine

And why shouldn't I be proud of my son, Robert?

Because you have to earn a son, Lamine. A son isn't like cash, an investment you put in a frozen bank account . . .

Okay! That's enough, Robert, shut up, Robert, leave me alone with my son . . . What do I say to him?

Nothing

What do you mean nothing?

What do you want to tell him?

What can you tell him?

What will you tell him?

Ah right! What will I tell him?

What do I want to tell him?

What do I have to tell him?

What should I say to the kid?

Lamine

Dad? Are you here to give me a hard time again? Aren't you sick of giving me a hard time?

My son, I came to stop this stupid war

Too bad! Because now we'll be bored my friend, oh yeah! We were always arguing or bored, right, dad? So let's move on now because honestly my head's full of tons more important things, so let's hear why you came back if it's not for a stupid argument?

I came to tell you to come back home

Is that all?

You are my son, Lamine

Oh yeah? That's news to me!

I want us to forget all that, to start a new life, I want you to come back home, to your home

My home?

Yes your home

And where is my home?

It's your home, the home that's yours and mine, it's where you were born, where your umbilical cord is buried, where you learned to walk, run, fall, pick yourself back up, smell, laugh, cry, fight, where your absence births a gaping hole in our hearts . . .

Wow! I don't recognize you, dad, shit you've become a poet! Have you been a poet for a while now, dad? No but seriously even Shakespeare couldn't come up with that: "where your absence births a gaping hole in our hearts!" Holy crap, what did it take to turn you into a poet? . . . Don't touch me! I'm not going anywhere because this is my home. It's where I learned to fall, pick myself back up, smell, do all the stupid things you just listed that in your opinion mean you have the right to a roof somewhere under this sky where angels won't stop getting drunk and pissing on us while God sleeps from sheer exhaustion because he wouldn't stop shouting at us: on your feet comrades, on your feet comrades, go comrades, on your feet, get together, like little red ants working together to lift an elephant's hip bone, be like ants, comrades, because the capitalists are conning you with TV, beer, tobacco, communitarianism, racial profiling, racism, nazism . . . and you're fighting each other, when you've already been beaten down by the rain of investments, of the government, of unchecked capitalism that pisses you off like you piss me off, dad, by coming back here, even though I'm good here, even though you're the one who kicked me out, just because I liked making toys with Robert, I wanted to dumpster dive with Robert, I wanted to glide across the sky like a migrating bird, I wanted Robert to teach me how to build a plane so I could make one for us, for you, for mom and me, so that with Robert we'd fly like doves off into the distance, but you didn't want to understand or listen to my dream. You'd say: "I don't want a stray dog in my house, if I see you again with that stray dog Robert, I'll throw you out", and that's what you did in the end, even though my scent, my laughter, my footsteps . . .

Lamine

Mom? What are you doing here, mom?

Bringing you

Bringing me? Where?

To our home

To our home?

Yes to our home

Where is our home, mom?

Your father's house. Your house

I don't like our home

You can only be at ease in our home, my son

Is that true, mom?

My son, we waited for you for so long

Waited?

Yes waited

Why did you wait for me, mom?

Everyone waits at some point. Everyone waits for a bit of bread. A bit of familiarity. A bit of a dream. A bit of sun. A bit of rain. A bit of land. A bit of peace. A bit of closeness. And when what we're waiting for doesn't arrive, we go looking for it. Everyone's waiting for my son. Everyone's waiting at the house, the café, the restaurant, in our hearts, in our bodies, in the sky . . . And when we expect the person we're waiting for not to come we lose patience we worry and minutes go by and days go by and months go by and we say to ourselves that we messed up with our son, our wife, our best friend, that we should've listened to him a little, been more indulgent, more understanding . . . we're sorry for treating him like he was trash, for throwing him out on the streets as if he wasn't flesh of our flesh . . .

I don't want people waiting for me, mom, sorry, I can't wait . . .

It's what we do for everyone, Lamine

I'm the exception to the rule, mom. No one should wait for me, I won't wait for anyone, I'm going, I'm going somewhere else, fresh air, fresh look, somewhere no one expects anything from me, where I don't expect anything from anyone, go, mom, because I'm not coming back, sorry, mom, but that's how it is, you know I never liked rules, so when she said, suddenly, like this, I don't have my period anymore, it was August ma'am, I was afraid of her period, her period that was mixing with the angel piss from the August sky, from then on someone was waiting for me in her belly . . .

No, mom, I won't go back, why are they waiting for me?

28 And If I Killed Them All, Ma'am?

What do they expect from me, mom?

To wait is to hope

Do you have some money, ma'am?

I don't have anything, mom, I swear I've got nothing, no hope, no house, no work but I've looked, ma'am, but you know how it goes, mom, no more work anywhere, who's to blame, the crisis, but who's the father of the crisis, mom, investments, mom, investments that only see us as as other investments and not as long-awaited hopes, as fathers, as long-awaited husbands, no mom

Hand over the bag, ma'am!

So no more time to build bridges of hope, of waiting, of humanity between you and me mom, no more love, but I love her, ma'am, that night, I didn't really leave that night, ma'am, when I'd gotten a few miles away something inside me began to fall like overripe fruit falls from a tree, something collapsed, coalesced, darkened, froze, something like Elephantiasis from the mosquitos growing inside me, on me, I couldn't keep moving, her audacious laughter, her explosive anger, her mysterious hands, her delicate face, I already missed everything about her intensely, I laughed, I laughed and I stopped, I turned around, I was thirty-something feet away from her, she was already asleep, in the middle of this starry, calm night, she was sleeping with the switchblade I'd given her held firmly in her right hand and her left hand on her belly, something made me stand still again . . .

Don't be afraid, Lamine, nothing's going to happen to her, to them, if that happens in a couple of weeks you'll be back, Lamine, you'll make a fortune for the kid and you'll come back and laugh with your little family, don't stay here, here there's only trash bags, rotten fruit, only flies piled up on banana peels, mango peels, only flesh burning in the sun, only cement trucks clogging up our lungs, only Kleenex filled with snot, only tears disappearing into the gutter, only wares hung around a twisting neck, only the legislature, only the mayors, only the presidential elections, dogs and vultures fighting over bones, only the smell of piss, only spit, only Made in China Made in Switzerland Made in Canada Made in the USA Made in France only shit here only only only . . .

So I said to myself: "you've seen how a hen is with her chicks? She scratches the ground all day for her chicks and before the sun rises she's up again with them, I didn't want to leave, but I had to be or not be. Be the dad who asks himself how and what his kid will eat today, be the dad who runs from his kid's worried, curious gaze, be the dad who asks himself why other people get to eat, drink, take care of themselves, have fun and not him . . . I didn't want to be that dad, I know that kind of dad, Robert's dad was that kind of dad, never home, never laughing with Robert, never giving Robert anything sweet, never celebrating Robert's birthday, always yelling at him, hitting him for nothing, hitting Robert's mom all the time all the time no . . . I didn't want to be like Robert's dad, so I looked at her asleep on our cardboard and I turned back around, and I ran ran ran

The light, Lamine

What about the light?

It's going to turn green

And?

And then the lady will have to leave, you're not the only one who knows how to leave, my man, everyone leaves some day, my friend . . .

Ma'am! Ma'am! Sorry, but now you need to tell me something, the light's turning green soon, and you'll have to leave, Robert says everyone leaves someday, so tell me before you leave what you would have done if you were in my shoes:

Leave?

Stay?

Do you think she's still waiting for me?

That she's expecting me?

Say something, ma'am, there's no time left and I need to be polite and greet you properly after all that, don't think I'm not polite, I'll greet you properly, ma'am, but if people were waiting for you, if you were the only hope for your son, your spouse, what would you have done, if as a Donzo, you didn't have any prey for your stew in your hunting bag? What would you have done if you'd promised your spouse to bring back a bit of hope from your trip but during your trip hope was just as scarce as work?

Absence

What would you do if only absence led to hope?

Say something, ma'am . . . because the blood the blood the blood, the smell of your blood, to taste your blood . . . say something, ma'am . . . a switchblade, a switchblade in the face of a lightning bolt sent down by a bastard from the August sky, your fucking Louis Vuitton, ma'am, your cash, what a joke, your cash, your car, open your car door . . . there are only a few more seconds left of the red light, and after, after, ma'am, you know what happens after, everyone behind you will start honking like crazy because people need to leave, why don't people want me to leave when every second is just movement? Departure? Flight? And who's waiting for us? Someone who's always been waiting for us my mom said, ma'am, who's waiting for you, ma'am? Your opinion, tell me your opinion . . . I see us, you and me, you and me alone, in a pool, in a pool filled entirely with blood, yours and mine and all of those people honking like idiots, and all of those people who look away, and all of those people who shut up . . . You really don't want to tell me what I should do? . . . but you have to tell me something, ma'am . . . because with all these idiots we're diving into our blood, we're smoking cigars, we're drinking champagne from glasses stamped Made in Emptiness and my switchblade, my switchblade in the face of the lightning bolt of the bastard from the August sky tears apart, tears me apart, tears apart all these idiots, you're crying, the idiots are crying and I'm drinking, I'm drinking your tears and don't look at me like that and Robert said there was a fucking million in your bag, show show show me what's in the bag and everything will be okay . . . because I don't want to wait here anymore, with all this black smoke sneaking out of tailpipes, no, ma'am, I can't wait here anymore, I want to leave too, so I'd say to myself like this, since you don't want to say anything, I'd say to myself like this, the cash, ma'am, I want the fucking cash . . . because I worked some, ma'am, I made planes and cars and motorcycles with milk cartons and other things like that and I sold them to tourists, over there tourists are only interested in art, ma'am, that's why Robert died, Robert the artist died of malaria, in August, there were no more tourists to buy Robert's art, tourists don't come in August, they're afraid of malaria, so Robert didn't have any money for malaria medication, so Robert left, ma'am, Robert went to be with the angels in the sky and piss on the earth in August, artists die quickly, ma'am, do you think I'm going to die ma'am, what do I do Robert? Robert? Mom? Dad? Robert? Ma'am?

No, ma'am, no more cash, I don't give a shit about cash, I'm sick of her, of him, of the emptiness ma'am, of the emptiness, so here's what I want: you, ma'am, you . . . no not you . . . your car . . . hahahaha!!! At the end of the day I want your car, with you inside, me next to you, no Louis Vuitton bag, no windshield wipers, no horn, no airbag, no cigarette lighter, you and me, you and me, not the idiots who run who run who run who honk, who don't give a shit, who fuck . . . you and me with cans all over your car, doves, your car stuffed with doves, with beer, with beer,

I'm the one paying, paying for the beer, you're driving, you're driving a thousand miles an hour, the kid has to be taken to school, his mom can't go to work in the sun . . . no music, no, no music . . . okay, alright . . . but only Robert's voice, Robert! Robert! . . . Your fucking bag! Where is your fucking Louis Vuitton with credit cards hidden in its slits? Where is it where is it where is it? . . . What are you doing, ma'am, stay in your car, I'm telling you to stay in your car, there are still a few more seconds of the red light, what do I do what do I do what do I do . . . don't be afraid . . . you know, ma'am, the Donzos are a hunting clan, apparently they can't come back from a hunt empty-handed, if that happens they have to offer up themselves as the prey, so they always find a way to bring something back from the hunt, I'm a Donzo, ma'am, a Donzo who's coming back from the hunt empty-handed, so I said to myself, but first I want to greet you properly, ma'am, that way we're square, ah! That's it, ma'am . . . I was wondering, ma'am, and if . . .

He takes out a gun.

Ear-piercing car horns. Insults fly . . . he raises the gun as the stage goes to black. Gunshot . . . Police siren. Ambulance siren . . .

Tears from the August Sky

Preface to *Tears from the August Sky*

By Ramatou Ouédraogo, star of the 2023 FARaway Festival Comédie de Reims production. Translated by Anna G. R. Miller.

Playing the role of this young girl who had to leave home to escape the pressure her parents put on her was both a challenge and an opportunity to push beyond what I knew myself capable of as an actor. I was very scared because it was the first time I performed solo on stage, my first production in another country (in France), and the role in and of itself was challenging . . . It takes time for all actors to embody a character, get inside the character; it takes a lot of work on a role to be able to embody it. And it was a bit challenging, especially since I was a young actor fresh out of theatre school . . . But, thanks to Aristide, who took his time explaining the text to me, illuminating it even further, and helping me really understand it . . . it took time but it became increasingly easy for me to embody it.

When I step into the role, I feel this pain, this desire to express myself, this hope and freedom . . . It gives me goosebumps and often, after the performance ends, it takes some time before I can leave the character behind. The text is so powerful, the words are so impactful, and above all else, her energy is so intense, it gives me goosebumps to embody her on stage.

2 Ramatou Ouedraogo in *Les larmes du ciel d'août* (*Tears from the August Sky*), directed by Aristide Tarnagda in 2023 for the FARaway Festival at the Comédie de Reims in France. Photo © Vincent VDH.

Tears from the August Sky

Translated by Anna G. R. Miller

Tears from the August Sky is a solo play written in monologue form depicting the unnamed pregnant girlfriend of Lamine, the protagonist of *And If I Killed Them All, Ma'am?* Standing at an intersection near where she and Lamine used to live together, the girlfriend responds to an unseen female driver who has stopped to offer help upon observing her advanced stage of pregnancy and seeming homelessness. Over the course of the monologue, she tries to persuade the driver to leave her where she stands, attempts to explain her refusal to leave by recalling her love of Lamine and complicated childhood, and ultimately brings new life into the world. The play was first performed in 2007 at the Récréâtrales Festival in Ouagadougou, Burkina Faso, and then traveled to the Avignon Festival later that year. A 2011 production that debuted in Kinshasa was also featured that year in the Festival les Francophonies in Limoges, France. Among other productions, the play was recently featured alongside *And If I Killed Them All, Ma'am?* in the 2023 Festival FARaway at the Comédie de Reims. The original French version (*Les larmes du ciel d'août*) was published by Lansman Editeurs in 2013. It has one female character.

Notes on the Translation: The original French edition includes a footnote after the term *non loti* explaining that this is a name given to the shantytown neighborhoods of Ouagadougou that have no paved streets, running water, or electricity and are composed of makeshift houses. The dedications in italics and epigraph are written by the playwright.

Characters

The girl

To Afi, Géné, Rabi, Aoula, and Marguo

To Assita

I knew a world

Drunk on trash

Where people led each other into the darkness

The king was named Filthy

Filthy married all the chicks on the block

As all looked on unmoved

From the bellies of whores fell street kids

Whose mouths didn't know how to spew out songs

They spit up only shit

And stained the world's dress with it

High noon. In the middle of the street. A car. A woman. A girl. And maybe . . .

The girl No, ma'am

Thanks

I'm waiting

I'm waiting for someone

My man

Thanks for your sympathy. I'll manage. Ever since he left I've managed on my own. I don't want help. I don't like handouts. Start your SUV and go . . . It's noon. Your son's waiting for you to come back so he can eat and take a nap, your husband's losing patience waiting to enjoy the meal, gulp down the beer, and fall asleep with his head in your lap. The housekeeper's imagining the worst possible scenarios because the lady of the house hasn't returned. They need you. You need your family, husband, housekeeper, your family. They need you. I don't need you. They're waiting for you. No one is waiting for me. I'm waiting. For his dad. My man. Do you get it?

Don't worry, he'll come. Come back . . .

I need him like they need you at home. It's not worth it to stay, ma'am. Right now the sun, the sky, they're vindictive. It's August, ma'am, and in August the sun, the sky, everything is vindictive. The sun scorches everything. The sky soaks everything with sudden tears. The August sky is like that, ma'am. Do you get it?

Go, ma'am, or else you're going to get scorched and soaked by the August sky and sun. It's not worth it to stay here. I'll always refuse to get in your car, go with you, accept your help. There's no point in insisting, in waiting. Do you get it?

No one is going to see you on TV, or in the newspapers. Helping a pregnant girl on the street isn't breaking news. It's banal. The world is full of bullshit like that. Do you get it?

There's no point in insisting, ma'am. I'm stubborn. I'm known for that. They've all tried like you. It didn't work. Get out of here and drive home. I don't like people helping me. I'm not on welfare or a street kid, I know how to manage . . . This is my home. I'm waiting for my guy, my man . . .

I said no no no and no, I'll wait here, everyone can wait where they want to wait, right? I'm waiting for my man here. He'll come back here. Our kid will be born here . . .

I'm telling you to go! I don't need you, you're starting to make me mad. And when I get mad I'm not nice and when I'm not nice it's not good . . .

It's none of your business. Do you know me? People help people they know, parents, kids, moms, cousins, uncles, dads, friends . . . I'm nothing to you, not even your friend. Do you get it?

Go, my man will come back . . . I don't know when but he'll come back. I have to wait here. That's all I know . . .

He didn't want to leave

To abandon us, his kid and me

But he had to leave

Because his kid, our kid, was waiting to come out

Do you get it?

He had to go get money

For our son

Money's important

Maybe our son won't want to live here like us. With us. He'll need money in that case. To buy himself a piece of land, to live there with his family, to build a sheet metal house or even a big house there. Everything will depend on his choice, on what he'll want to have or be. Right? That's why he left, ma'am . . .

One night, while we were gazing up at the stars that light the sky with their white teeth after making love, because every night we made love, well one night when we were gazing up at the sky, he walked his fingers along my belly and said to me:

Our kid's coming soon. I have to go get money for him.

He won't need any. So you don't need to go, my man.

It's not such a sure thing. It's our kid, not us. You never know. He might like money. I don't want him to be sad because we wanted him to be like us.

You're right.

So I have to go. I don't know where. Maybe far from here or nearby. Let's hope I can find some money for our kid there. Don't worry. Don't move. Wait for me here. I'll come back here and find you. Here's my twelve punches knife, if someone bothers you, give him my twelve punches to the stomach. Don't let anyone take you away from here. I want to come back and find you here. You got it?

Yes . . .

You won't move after I go?

Never. I'll wait for you here, all my life. I won't let anyone move me from here. Go, don't worry. You'll find me here. Maybe with our kid. I'll wait for you . . .

Then I took this twelve punches and took a blood oath. I cut my finger. Blood spurted out. I drank from it . . .

If you don't come back here and find me, let the blood I've just put in my stomach become a clot in my belly and suffocate me.

I was afraid he didn't believe me, didn't believe he'd come back and find me and his son. He took the switchblade and cut his finger too, drank from the blood that spurted out of his finger . . .

If I don't come back here and find you, you and our kid, may my blood become a venom as virulent as the viper's and . . .

You don't have to swear. I did it to reassure you . . .

And I devoured his lips. Took off his clothes and took off mine. Our bodies became one as the jubilant stars in the sky watched on. The exquisite pleasure that pumped blood into every part of our bodies closed our eyes in spite of the vrooming of the cars and the chatter from the night owls . . .

In the morning he was already gone. The first seconds of solitude began to tick in my head . . . Do you get it?

I can't leave here. I promised to wait for him here with our kid. I'll wait. However long it takes. So I won't leave here. Don't waste your time . . .

I said no. Keep driving and leave me alone . . . If he dies . . . If I die, it's not your problem or anyone else's.

My man will come back and bury us. At least he'll know that I didn't betray him, that I kept my word . . .

Go, I'm going to get mad, I can stand you being here even less than I can stand what you're saying, I don't like it when people make me do things I don't want to do.

That's why I left the minister

My dad

The lawyer

My mom

They made me go to sleep at eight o'clock, drink coffee in the morning, brush my teeth, bathe three times a day, sweep and tidy my room, watch TV on vacation, take pocket money, go to school, only play with other ministers' and lawyers' kids, and on and on. It made me mad . . . They wanted me to be a lawyer and a minister's kid . . . Do you get it? They made me be like that. I didn't want that.

I wanted to be something else. I didn't want to be the minister's kid, or the lawyer's kid, or the rich one's kid, or the poor one's kid

I didn't want to be anything at all

I wanted to be a kid

Only a kid

Just a kid

Then a girl

Nothing but a girl

And a mom

No more than a mom

Do you get it?

I didn't want anything other than that. But the lawyer always wanted me to wear shoes. "Wear your shoes! What's that? You want to roughen up your toes so you look like a street kid? Huh?" she would go on and on about my toes when I refused to wear shoes.

My dad always cared about driving me to school so I didn't get beat up, even though I wanted to get beat up, I wanted to be black and blue all over . . . Do you get it?

It's because they forced me that I'm here

Waiting for this man

His kid in my belly

Here

Because he told me to wait here

This is where we took a blood oath not to betray each other . . .

Do you get it?

Yes?

I know you get it, you get me . . . But you're a mom and that's what's keeping you here. I get you, you know. Yes yes, I get everyone. But I want you to go because I'm not ever going to go with you in your car . . . I love this man too much to go with you. He's everything to me. You're a mom, you ought to get that.

Love!

Your heart's twin!

He's everything to us

Even if he's invisible to everyone else

Even if his body's just a dirty shell

We're attached to him

We wouldn't betray him for anything in the world

Right?

You see we get each other. So I'm begging you, go and let me wait.

You're putting yourself in danger here

We're on the streets here

The streets are a dangerous place

You shouldn't be here

People could beat you up

Make you black and blue all over

That's no good for rich people and you, you're rich

44 Tears from the August Sky

The streets are capable of anything ma'am

They can dent your beautiful car. Steal your bag, phone, anything and everything ma'am, like my man who left, the streets can attack you. Even me right here, in front of you, I can get you in the stomach with the twelve punches . . .

The streets are capable of anything ma'am. Go before they get mad . . . I'm begging you on my knees, your kids are already worried, your husband, the housekeeper, me right here because I can't stand you anymore. And I'm capable of anything once I can't stand things anymore. Believe me. I killed a lot of people, the night right after my guy left . . . I killed five men. They wanted to rape me. I got them in the guts with the twelve punches. And I took them far away from here. You must have heard about it on TV and on the radio, five men found gutted . . . Right? I killed them all. Because they wanted to force me. So, go, I don't want to kill you. You're putting yourself in danger here . . . Don't worry about me. I'll get by . . . You see? Traffic's heavy. People are going home. You could get yourself beat up if you stay here. Everyone's driving badly. There are a lot of accidents here. That's why the minister drove me to school. Go, please. The sky is getting darker. It's August.

I already told you in August the sky is vindictive. It cries and soaks everything with its tears . . .

Go

Getting soaked by tears from the August sky isn't good

It gives you the chills

Malaria

A cold

Get back in your car, get out of here, drive home. You're going to get soaked and it's not good for you. Your kids are going to be sad like the August sky and they'll cry nonstop. You love your kids, I'm sure of it. Like the lawyer loved me. All moms are like that.

I get it but you need to go, sprint off in your car, the sky is getting sadder and sadder. You'll see, it'll soak us instantly with its tears. The sky is like that in August. I'm telling you to get out of here, don't you see how everyone's running? Everyone's looking for somewhere they can avoid tears from the August sky . . .

Please ma'am, go, go back to your home. You're too pretty to be letting tears from the August sky get you all dirty, I'm begging you . . .

No! Don't bring that up again, I won't move. This is my home, you're reminding me, I'm going to put my things somewhere safe from the rain. In August, everyone's afraid of tears from the sky . . .

Drops of rain . . .

Are you still here?

What did I tell you?

The sky started to send us its tears

Get back in your car, at least you'll be protected there

No no no you think I'm an idiot?

I won't get into your car

You want to take me with you?

No?

Then why do you want me to get in?

No, that . . .

Thanks, I'm used to tears from the sky

I drink them and wash with them

Not at all, you get used to it

At the beginning it was hard but eventually my system adapted to it

More and more drops of rain . . .

Ah! The August sky is crying harder and harder

I warned you

But why are you waiting to get back in your car and go?

You're going to get soaked, you and your papers . . . Those papers are important! Put them in the car at least! Don't play with papers, ma'am, they're really essential, papers . . . They get you everything, health, future, housing, love, trips, family, identity, culture, race, status, and so on and so forth . . . If you don't have your papers you're fucked, you die unidentified, everyone avoids you, chases you away, you become dangerous like the streets . . .

Don't you get it?

Put these papers back in your car

I don't want you to become

A danger

A street

Because of me

People will walk all over you, shit on you, spit, piss on you . . .

Don't you hear me?

She pulls out the switchblade . . .

Put these papers back in the car or I'll gut you!

I'm not kidding

You see, there's nobody still stuck in traffic

It's just the two of us here

They all found somewhere safe to avoid tears from the August sky

What?

I didn't hear?

Okay, I'll get in with you

On the condition that you hand over the car keys

Okay

Hurry up, the papers are getting wet, give me your bag. Don't worry, I don't want to steal anything, I don't know how to do it . . . What? Speak up, I'm going deaf from the August sky tremolo . . . I want to see if you've got another key with you.

She searches the bag . . .

Okay, just some makeup . . . Give me the keys, go around the other side . . . I want to be in the driver's seat, that way I'm sure you won't take me with you, don't even try it, or else I'll have to get you in the stomach with my man's twelve punches . . .

She opens the car door and gets in . . .

Go to the other side

She opens the other car door . . .

Go quickly

She closes the car door

There, now your papers won't get washed out by tears from the sky

It's pretty, huh!

Your car?

Are you the one who bought it?

Your husband?

He's nice, huh!

Was it a wedding gift?

Have you been married for a long time?

It's good, you've got to get married when you're in love, right?

You're happy, right?

That's what's most important

You know, my man and me we're going to get married when he comes back . . . We decided before he went to get money . . . Do you think our son will need money? Huh? You don't know . . . It's no big deal, you don't have to know everything. We're on the streets here not in school, we don't have to know anything . . .

But I think, or I hope that he doesn't need any, and even if he needs some that he won't go crazy over it and get greedy and evil.

You know my dad and my mom loved money so much they didn't make love at night like my man and me . . .

They liked counting money more

My dad would tell my mom how much money he'd embezzled from his ministry

My mom would say how much she'd snatched from the account of whatever client she'd gotten exonerated that day

I was still small

Ten years old maybe

I don't remember anymore

But every night, after the housekeeper thought I was asleep, I liked to leave my room and put my ear up to the lawyer and minister's door . . . I was curious, that's all . . .

I wanted to hear what parents could say to each other when they were alone

But every night it was the same as it is on the streets

The counting

The money

And that always made me mad

Do you do that with your husband every night too?

Oh! Sorry, I'm very curious

My man always gave me a hard time about that

Do you think he's not coming back?

Honestly?

It's been six months since he left

Maybe more, I'm not counting anymore, so I don't feel the weight of the time on my shoulders

No

I didn't move

No

Because I'm telling you I have to wait for him here

No no . . .

And if I move and he gets here after me, would he think I'd betrayed him?

No no no . . .

He'd do something stupid

I don't know, for example

Kill himself

Lose hope

Losing hope is worse than death, you know?

Yes

I've stayed here ever since and haven't moved

Yes yes . . .

Even if I move it's just to go to the side

Yes yes yes . . .

Did you see that hole over there? There it is, over there, I go just over there to shit and pee . . . I don't give a shit, who doesn't shit and pee? The police don't come by there, anyway I'm not afraid of them, I've got my man's twelve punches . . .

How do I eat?

People give me food!

Well, people like you!

People who think I'm begging!

You know, people think everything of everyone

What do I think of you?

Nothing at all

Because I like thinking nothing of people!

And you?

What do you think of me?

That's not true

You don't think I'm crazy, that I'm on welfare, or a penniless orphan, you don't think I'm crazy for having left the lawyer and the minister to come live like a stray on the streets, getting soaked by tears from every month's sky, getting myself fucked and knocked up by dogs like my man, sleeping, peeing, shitting in the gutters, stuffing myself with people's crumbs, gnawing at peoples' consciences by making them pity me . . .

You don't think all that deep down inside of you, when you saw me, you said to yourself "oh! Lord Jesus, Mary Mother of God, what crazy fly must have bitten this girl to make her like that on the streets! Well then! Apparently we're going to see everything in the world nowadays! She must be a whore, an addict, a reject . . . for sure . . . And then the thugs there didn't even take pity on her, they fucked her until they knocked her up . . . for sure . . ."

You didn't think all of that when you saw me? When you hit the brakes and got out of your car . . . You didn't think all of that when I told you I wouldn't follow you, when I told you I was waiting for my man, especially when I talked to you about the lawyer and the minister . . . You didn't think all of that? Don't be afraid to say it! You've got the right to think whatever you want! They say this is a democracy . . . so everyone can think whatever they want . . .

What do you think of me?

Nothing?

You don't want to talk anymore?

I'm bothering you?

Is that it?

So?

Why are you being quiet all of a sudden and looking at me like that?

I'm not pretty?

It's because I'm not wearing makeup anymore

Wait, let me borrow your makeup kit . . . Is it in the bag? I'm going to put on makeup, you'll see I'm pretty . . .

She takes the bag, takes out the makeup kit, opens it, looks in the rear-view mirror, and puts on makeup . . .

There you have it

Look at me now

I'm beautiful, right?

You see, right?

Actually there's no such thing as beautiful women or handsome guys, there's just good makeup, that's what my man always says . . . That's true, right?

Oh! I've got to pee

Wait for me

I'm coming back

Right away

Don't go, okay!

I'm just going to pee in the hole over there and I'll come back

Wait for me the August sky is still soaking everything

It's less cold in your car

And it's somewhere safe for both of us now

And we're keeping each other company

I need you now

Like my man

I'm falling in love with you

Don't look away like that, I'm not trying to fuck you, I mean I'm getting attached to you, from talking, having you near me, I think of you as a friend, you got it now?

Okay, good. It's always good when people get it. Okay, I'm going, or else I'm going to pee my pants and ruin your car . . .

Don't go, the August sky hasn't finished whining yet.

She gets out, runs, comes back to talk . . .

I'm just coming back to put down the keys, don't touch them! I brought them back because they could fall in the hole and tears from the sky will take them away, tears from the sky take everything in the holes . . . Are you listening?

Okay, I'll be back in two seconds

I just need to take off my shorts

And empty my bladder

Okay?

She runs, gets to the hole, takes off her shorts, crouches . . .

Don't shake your head

Nobody can see me

They're all safe in houses

You?

It's no big deal, I'm not ashamed, we've all got the same holes, only mine's bigger because my man likes to make love to me every night. He likes that.

Just like

The lawyer

The minister

Like to count money every night

Everyone has something they like

Does your husband like to make love to you every night?

Okay, it's okay, I'm sorry, I'm being rude . . .

She gets back up, puts her shorts back on, looks at the hole for a long time . . .

The sky cried a lot, its tears filled up the hole and they're carrying everything to other holes, ditches definitely, maybe dams . . .

The August sky is like that, when it starts to cry it doesn't know how to stop. Maybe it doesn't realize it's soaking everything and carrying away papers, animals, trash, trees, streets, plastic bags, sheds, Kleenex, trash cans . . . There are some days when it's so sad it cries a whole day more . . .

It's true!

There are days like that

Days when the August sky cries

As if it wanted its tears to drain the shit

Down to the mouths of the alligators and the fish

There are days like that

Days like that when the August sky soaks you so completely with its tears that you want to disappear, as if you were a sad painting, an outline, a stick figure drawn by a toddler . . . Yes, ma'am, I'm sure, it's because you're never outside when the August sky cries, or else there are days when you'd think it was vindictive, it cries so much those days that you want to slap the bastard making it cry so much and stab the jerk who threw you out on the streets and into the wrath of the tears, punish the kid who drew you so badly, who made you look like a painting nobody would want to buy, swallow up the person who made you invisible, illiterate . . .

Yes, ma'am

There are days like that

Days when my man and I, we wish we had a hideaway to crawl into when the August sky cries nonstop like right now.

Days like that when this bastard of an August sky pushes the gutters until they overflow, because it's through the gutters that Morpheus comes to stuff us full of pipe dreams . . .

She turns toward the car . . .

Don't worry, ma'am

I'm coming

I'm used to being soaked by tears from the August sky

I got in your car to make you happy

To stop your papers from getting soaked

To help you avoid

Malaria

The cold

A cold

Do you get me?

Don't worry, I'll be right back

I'm thinking about my man

Maybe somewhere tears from the August sky are lashing him

He might be cold

He definitely wants to make love

He wants me to hold him in my arms and chase away the cold

Maybe he's wandering around looking for a sky where the August sky will be miles away

Since I'm miles away right now

Since I'm not there to spread my legs for him

Since I'm not there to wrap my arms around him

Do you get it?

He's withering away right now at the mercy of the August sky

He could've been in your car and avoided tears from the sky

Do you think someone like you will care about him?

Someone like you will open their car door for him?

Someone will find him a bed?

Is that true?

Oh! If I could talk to that person like you, I would tell them: "thank you, my brother, my sister, thank you for shielding my man from tears from the August sky, don't worry about the mess about the bed. It's not your fault, it's the weather that's sad. Don't mope around if there are puddles in the shack because we adapted to the gutters without it even messing up our sleep. If he's looking for somewhere now it's because the weather's vindictive and the sky cries all the time, that's why my man's off to somewhere else . . . Bring him somewhere even if it's to a tent city or a *non loti* shantytown, as long as he takes shelter . . ."

I'd tell them that, ma'am

She goes toward the car, it's raining less and less . . .

You can go now, ma'am

The August sky is quieting down

It's getting tired of crying or its tears are stopping

Start your car and go

Your husband, your kids, the housekeeper, the boss, are worried

They're afraid, they think you got beat up, that tears from the sky carried you off in the gutters, maybe they're in mourning, maybe they're hoping to hear about you on the radio, they're waiting for news from you, they're all waiting for you like I'm waiting for my man . . .

Go, ma'am, because I won't leave here

Thanks for giving me somewhere safe to be and for understanding

Go on

I'm waiting

I'm waiting for him

Like they're waiting for you

Go and reassure your family

Go quickly, the sky might get sad again now

It's unpredictable in August, you know

Go I'm begging you

Maybe you'll see my man

On the drive

Bring him here

Or tell him I'm still waiting for him here

Where he made love to me every day

Where we drank each other's blood

Where I was supposed to wait for him with our kid

Tell him to run run run

Without running out of breath

Because I'm running out of breath waiting for him

To be taken out by acid tears from the August sky

Tell him I love him

Tell him I crave his body

Tell him even if he doesn't have our kid's money

He should come back

Our kid will get it

He's waited too long for him too

He wants to come out now

In a few minutes he won't be able to wait for him anymore

Of course he can't wait as long as me

Right, ma'am?

So, go on, start your car

Don't cry, you shouldn't cry

Stop spilling your tears like the sky

I don't like people who cry

It does nothing to cry

Take your car and get out of here

Bring my man back instead of crying

Do it quickly, our son's coming out, he's tired of waiting for his daddy. I told you he can't wait for him any longer. You didn't listen to me and now he's mad and . . .

Flow

Flow

Flow

Flow like tears from the sky . . .

Look how beautiful he is

He looks like my man

Same parts, he's his spitting image

He looks just like him!

I'm so happy

When he comes back he won't worry I cheated on him with someone else

He won't get mad

He won't yell like when he sees me with another guy

He's really jealous, you know

Go . . .

She cleans her thighs . . .

I'm going to keep him in a bag

That way he'll see him when he comes back

No, no, don't get out of your car again

I'll manage

Don't bother

It's cold outside the car

It's always like that when the sky finishes crying

Go now

When I've finished picking up our kid and I've put him in a bag, I'm going to wash myself in the ditch . . .

After a birth, you have to wash yourself, right?

Do you see?

I'm already a mother!

You thought I was a kid, right?

She opens the car door . . .

A kiss goodbye

Okay pass me my man's twelve punches

Now's when I need it most

Now that our kid is here

I have to protect him until he comes back

She closes the car door . . .

Now go . . .

I'll wait here

Maybe you'll see my man on the way

Maybe he's tired of walking

Maybe lost

Maybe . . .

Bring him

I miss him

He misses me

But the weather, and the distance, and the August sky make us lose our way . . .

Drive quickly

Thanks for giving me somewhere safe to be

Thanks for everything . . .

Now go

It'll be night soon

And at night

The streets are dark

The August sky gets sad

And everything becomes

Night

Night

Night . . .

Red Earth

Preface to *Red Earth*

By Kiswend-sida Urbain Guiguemdé, who starred in the 2021 Theater Stok (Zurich) production. Translated by Anna G. R. Miller.

As a Burkinabè actor and musician living in Switzerland, *Red Earth* led me to think about the kinds of relationships people who leave their homeland have with each other, whether living abroad or immigrating to a new country, and the challenge of maintaining contact with family and friends. Because when we are far from the eyes of the people we love, we rely on messages and social media, in spite of every kind of internet issue you could imagine taking place. We don't let go. After some bouts of loneliness in spite of the fact that I had family with me in Zurich, I learned how to live another life, in a new culture, with new customs, and a different sense of humor. I had some sleepless nights for several years. I often found myself out on my balcony, after having left the bed where my wife lay sleeping. Because at night, it was as if I found myself surrounded by friends, hanging out in the house where I grew up (my parents' house) and where the idea of leaving began running through my mind. Still to this day, I ask myself: Who truly leaves? Why do we always want to reminisce? Can you leave somewhere without really leaving it behind? Can your body separate from your soul? Why are we so attached to our childhood? When do we leave? Do we leave with our battles, our struggles? Do we leave because we dropped out of a fight? What do the people we left behind expect from us, do they really assume all foreigners are trying to make money so they can bring it with them when they go back to their homeland? The people who stayed put, are they just waiting for us to send back money? Don't they need more than that? Is it easy to return the way we came? As time passes, we change too.

During the European productions of this play, many people approached me after the show to share childhood nostalgia, others told me stories their parents used to tell them when they were kids and talked about how much the world has changed since then. Many older people came up to me and told me about their childhood during the independence movements of the 1960s. Many found themselves without a land to call their own.

3 Kiswend-sida Urbain Guiguemdé in *Terre Rouge* (*Red Earth*), directed by Miriam Lustig in 2021 at Theater Stok in Zürich, Switzerland. Photo © Christina Steybe.

Red Earth

Translated by Heather Jeanne Denyer

Red Earth is a solo play that depicts two brothers—one who left for Europe and one who remained in Africa—reflecting back on their shared memories of childhood on the red earth of their homeland through a series of letters. They share moments of their separate lives as adults, their hopes, and the realities that keep those hopes out of reach. The play was developed with the Bottom Theatre and commissioned by the Festival les Francophonies in Limoges, France, where it premiered in 2012. It had a reading at the Avignon Theatre Festival and was performed at the Festival de la Luzège in Saint-Pantaléon-de-Lapleau, France, both in 2013. It was also featured in 2015 at the Théâtre National Populaire in Villeurbanne, France. More recent productions include one in 2021 at the Theater Stok in Zurich, Switzerland. Along with *Ways of Loving*, it won ADELF's 2018 *Grand prix littéraire d'Afrique noire* (Best African Literary Work, awarded by the French-Language Writers' Association). The original French version (*Terre rouge*) was published by Lansman Editeurs in 2017. The play has two male characters often performed by one actor.

Notes on the Translation: The French text has been translated, but the original Bissa in the play has been left intact; it is italicized. Bissa is one of sixty-six Indigenous languages spoken in Burkina Faso. It is the language spoken by the Bissa, a people of Mande ethnic origins, and one of over sixty ethnic groups in Burkina Faso.

Characters

Two Brothers

Kon kaabr daa biideèma huunsu maan
Kon kaabr daa n'ziidaar maan
Kon kaabr daa kuupela maan
Kon kaabr daa wèla maan
Kon kaabr daa suunmaa taalaa maan
Kon kaabr daa suunmaa guenoonmaa
Koon kaabr daa n'zee huunsu maan
Kon kaabr daa n'zee maan
Kon kaabr daa n'naan huunsu maan
Kon kaabr daa n'naan maan
Kon kaabr daa duunyaan léo yuunoon maan

The graves are sealed

The mosquitoes abandon the corpses

The dogs abandon their watch

An explosion of dew on the grass

An explosion of hesitant voices

The moon disappearing

Dreams fading

Steps emerging

Splashes of water falling from faces

Hands grasping brooms

Voices of goats who run

Voices of hens who fall from their perches

Voice of a mule who wants to return to the grass

Voices of cows who await the shepherd

Drip

Drip

Drip

Red Earth

The earth drips with shadow

The sky drips with the sight of the day

The trees drip with the harmattan winds

Space drips with voices

The voices of babies

Voices of children

Voices of men

Voices of women

Aa dôkatii baba

Aa dôckatti n'naan

Aa dôckatti n'kiièsôr

I dôcktakii n'daanè

My brother

My earth

My earth is red

The harmattan bleaches lips

My red earth is full

Of grapes

Of locust beans

Of jujube trees

Of shea trees

Of carp

Of sardines

Of grasshoppers

Of lizards

Of cats

Of rats

Of mice
On my red earth

Girls soften their lips and feet with shea butter
Men drink *dolo* and *zoomkom* and beer and cola

The face of my brother
The face of my red earth

I see my brother's face in the face of my red earth
I see my brother's smile in the trees of my red earth
I smell my brother in the fields of my red earth
My brother left for France

One morning

The earth
The earth that holds my story
The earth that holds my dead
The earth that holds the trees, the flowers, the mountains, the waters
The earth that holds my home, our homes
The earth that holds my childhood
The earth that nursed my childhood
The earth that drank my saliva and my blood on the soccer fields
The earth where my embryo was embedded
My red earth

My brother sent me a letter
It was raining

I love when it rains on this red earth
Not because the sun is absent
Not because the trees grow green

Not because the toads croak

Not because the dragonflies fill the sky

Not because the flowers bloom

I love when it rains on my red earth

Because after the rain, a sweet scent nourishes my entire body

A scent of life fills our lungs after every rain on our red earth

When it rains on my red earth, the scent of life released from the earth resuscitates the mosquitoes. With mosquitoes in the houses, in the fields, in the wells, it's impossible for us not to catch a nasty disease. Despite the warm weather, our bodies would become extremely feverish and overcome by aches. Our mothers would send our brothers who weren't yet sick to pick the leaves of the lemon trees, papaya trees, mango trees, mahogany trees. Our mothers would boil these different leaves and make us drink them and breathe them in and bathe in them. By the end of the third day, we'd regain our spirits and our smiles stolen by the mosquitoes.

When I was little, when I stubbed my toe playing soccer or falling down, my brother would brush the dirt off with his hand. He would gather fine sand and cover my wound with it. A few days later, my wound would be healed.

My red earth and my brother were doctors!

In my red earth, when my brother and I were hungry, we wouldn't cry, we wouldn't go scraping the bottom of pots. When my brother and I were hungry, my brother would look me in the eyes and I would take his hand and we would go out. Outside, we would find mango trees and guava trees. My brother would climb up the trees and from the top of the mango and guava trees he would let mangoes and guavas fall into my empty stomach. The outside filled our stomachs. Then, when our stomachs were full, my brother would leap from the treetops into my arms and with him in my arms, I would run straight to the Wèla, the river that sings with the mango and guava trees. As soon as I got to the bank of the Wèla, I would throw him in the water before I jumped in right after. Right away, my brother would start splashing me with water, and I would splash him, too. The splashes of water caressed the mangoes and guavas lodged in the bottom of our guts; then we'd be tired and my brother would look at me and I'd take him in my arms again and we would go lie down.

One morning, a bunch of people showed up with a bunch of machinery; one morning when the air had deposited vigor on all the kids' faces; kids who like monkeys or cats jumped from one mango tree to another, from one shea tree to another, from one grasshopper to another, from one lizard to another, and this bunch of machinery arrived from the government they said, my brother began to cry and all the other children began to scream. The machinery's racket broke the silence provided every morning by the dew. The pulse of the wind took on a crazy rhythm, and all around us, the machines and the cries were swept away with the tempest, and it all overwhelmed me. I didn't know where I was anymore, where to go with all this confusion, what do you become when your childhood falls like a rotten mango into the river? When suddenly 100 years is shoved in your face? When the silence begins its deafening scream in your ears? I began to scream at my brother and the others and the ululating machines, yet on my red earth, the silence was already buried. Then I began to run in all directions and my brother and the others did, too. But everywhere there was mourning for the silence. The government machines had swept it all away. And I told my brother and the other kids to shut up because there was no more point in screaming. Why scream when the silence is dead?

Since my brother left for France, all he sends is letters

Letters

Letters

Letters

I'm afraid of opening this letter

I'm afraid of reading it

My brother's letter doesn't smell like the red earth after the rain

It smells like dust

It smells like the Harmattan

It smells like a cold

It smells like a cough

Since my brother left

Since the government machines got here

There's nothing left but the smells of colds and coughs

The shadowy smells

No more shea trees

No more jujubes

No more locust beans

No more sheep pens

No more Harmattan

No more smells of red earth

No more life

No more death

My brother writes:

> I am still in Paris
>
> In a bar
>
> It's cold
>
> A sports bar
>
> A lot of people in the bar
>
> People drinking and watching soccer
>
> Do you still play soccer, bro?
>
> The metro
>
> Another life in Paris
>
> An underground life
>
> The metro hisses
>
> I like the sound of the metro
>
> You'd like it, too
>
> I'd love to let you listen to the sound of the metro
>
> Over the phone
>
> But you don't like phones
>
> You wouldn't let me send you a phone
>
> You wouldn't let me send you a TV

Maybe you would have seen me

Seen me again

If there was a TV at home?

Maybe I would have seen you

Seen you again

If you had accepted the TV?

People get off the metro

To wander around probably

In Paris, nothing to do but wander around

To wander alone

To wander into cafés, bars, metro stations, to the Eiffel Tower, Montparnasse, Belleville,

Chateau Rouge . . .

To wander among the billboards that flood the metro stations

To wander in the dead of winter

To wander into the honking cars

To wander into the cops' guns

I wander, too

In you

In all of you

I wander in you walking under the corrosive sun

I wander in your body covered in the dust of soccer fields

I wander in your faraway laughter

I wander in your wounds that lack red earth to heal them

I wander in you sitting down for tea

Watching the girls in the road

Spewing trifles at the girls

Screaming at the kids who want to cross the roads

Playing cards, checkers, Parcheesi

The metro

The metro hisses

It's going somewhere else

To another neighborhood of Paris no doubt

Me, I'm staying

I'm staying in the sports bar

I just ordered another beer

The fifth

Rest assured

It's my last beer

My last cigarette

Normally I don't drink this much

Today, I'm letting myself go

Hey! Don't worry too much about the cigarette, you're the one who infected me with that. Do you remember? We were hiding in an okra field with an ember. We broke a dry okra pod, which we lit with the ember. A whitish smoke rose from the pod. You took two, three drags, then you made me take a drag, too. And we started wheezing like goats. And our eyes turned red . . .

How are your eyes now?

In Paris, there are many mirrors, many windows, many books, many people who spend their time looking at themselves in the many mirrors, the many windows, and the many books, and I'm writing to you in a sports bar, bro. There are a lot of people drinking and watching soccer. Me, I can't watch soccer. I cough. I wheeze like when we were in the okra fields. I wheeze, bro. More and more every day. Don't worry. It's not too bad. Just a few streams of blood I sometimes cough up. But you, you know that I've got enough blood to give away. Just a few bits of lung mixed in with the stream of blood my chest expels. But you, you know that we are the lungs. It's nothing. It must be the cigarette. But I promise you this is the last one. Soon we'll be together. Soon. Don't tell anyone. Not even mom and dad. I want it to be a surprise. As soon as I get home . . . here, in Paris, I mean, I'll pack my bags. All my bags will be full. You'll see. I thought of everything. I looked for everything. The government with its machines will get the fuck out when I get there. Soon we'll be together, bro. I'm happy in this bar. This sports bar. The match is over. People are emptying their glasses. They're not celebrating. The match was a blowout. No goals. I'm having my last cigarette outside. The next metro. I'll come with a metro in my suitcase. The metro hisses. People have finished emptying their glasses. They're going home. It'll be soon for me, bro. I watch the metro leave again going elsewhere. I want to catch it, to fold it in four, and to shove it in the bottom of my bag. If at least the government instead of machines, billboards, satellites, obnoxious mansions, traffic lights, Chinese mopeds, privatized factories, Canadians, Chinese, French, Americans, had installed metros for us. People wouldn't have to go to work under the angry sun. People wouldn't have to go to the hospital in pushcarts. Women wouldn't have to fray their hair carrying bundles of sticks on their heads and wouldn't have to sleep on the road. Children wouldn't have to let themselves be cursed by four-by-fours, by Renaults, by Land Cruisers, or other stupid things eating away our lives. But don't worry, brother. I'm coming. I'm leaving the bar. It's really cold. The bar's closing. The metro isn't hissing any more. I just put out my last cigarette. The streets are empty. The bits of lung and trickles of blood keep me company. Paris is beautiful at night. Beautiful in its silence. Beautiful with its stores and their windows. Beautiful with its streets filled with drunk people. Beautiful with drunk, carefree people. Beautiful with cigarette smoke that covers the dark clouds. Paris is beautiful but I can't do it anymore. So let me light a cigarette. One for the road. To not be alone with my bits of lungs and trickles of blood. Please, brother, let me light one, the bar is empty, no more soccer, the metro's sleeping, the night is there and my lungs, my lungs, my lungs, and leave me the fuck alone with your reproaches and your morality because you, yourself know that I wouldn't want that. You know very well that I didn't want to be there, at that Koltesienne time of night, with my lungs and my trickles of blood, but the goddamn government with those damned machines, but you, you knew Cheikh Hamidou Kane and his *Ambiguous Adventure* and his Most Royal Lady and his ability to conquer without being right and his desire to bind wood with wood. And I love Wole Soyinka with his tiger who doesn't proclaim its tigritude but jumps on its prey. Needed to leap and I leapt, I leapt and I regret nothing, so leave me in peace and be happy doing what I ask you to. No one cares about my lungs, my trickles of blood are laughable, there's more important things, bro, I promise you there's more important things, take a good look in my bags, in each one of them there's money, money for school, money for solar panels, money for water, money for vegetable gardens, money for the hospital, money so that no government will have any pretext to come and cause trouble with us without fair warning. Build schools quickly. Send all the kids there. Girls just like boys. Invent a written form of our language. They need to speak and write our language. That's the only way we'll be respected. Teach them the governmental language, too. So that they know how to respond to governments. Because those who don't know how to respond to the oppressor are doomed to let themselves be oppressed, all the other stuff, bro, all the other stuff, it's old, man, forget it and do what I ask of you, I can feel that I've exhausted my lungs and my trickles of blood, I dragged them too much through the streets of Paris, so I need to rest, bro, in any case, no choice, all the bars are closed and soon it's going to rain, after the rain, the rain, the rain, the cold, the cold, the cold and the cold here, bro, it stings, it stings the skin, it stings in the rain. So a last cigarette to help the little bit of lung and the little blood I have left to drag home. Just enough time to open the door, to put cash in the envelope, and to figure all that out tomorrow morning. Just one more for the road, bro . . . Even if the cough's started up again . . . Goddamn cough, goddamn blood . . . You won't have me, I belong to my earth, I belong to my brother . . . Don't worry, bro, in France you always make it . . . Despite the cold and the rain . . . I'll make it, despite our suspicious looks . . . I'll be there, in spite of the lungs and the trickles of blood that quit on us . . . despite the siren that's going off . . . don't worry, bro . . . I'm home and my saliva just sealed the envelope . . . the siren . . . I hear a siren, bro . . . Do you hear the siren, bro? Don't worry . . . soon . . . soon I'll be with you, with all of you . . . despite the siren, despite the silence . . . your silence . . .

My earth.

My earth was red.

Now my earth is black.

My brother

My brother's feet were always covered in shit from kids and dogs

Because my brother liked to run barefoot over the tufts of grass

Every morning, my brother would hide to watch the naked girls

Because every morning the girls would get naked in the grass drunk with dew

They threw themselves in the grass drunk with dew to enjoy the embrace of the dewdrops

Now my brother is a letter

Now my brother is a phone call

Fucking government

Fucking machines that transform my brother into words

Distant words

Words without echoes. Words that want to collect the water that's already in the earth. Because there, bro, I really love you, but here there's nothing left but a parentheses of blood as Sony Labou Tansi put it. And in Sony's parentheses of blood, everything is in the earth. Grass in the earth. Laughter in the earth. Trees in the earth. Fields in the earth. Respect in the earth. The elderly in the earth. Women in the earth. Stories in the earth. Dancing in the earth. Blood in the earth. Language in the earth. Silence in the earth. Everything in the earth.

So what do you want me to do with your money since everything is already in a parentheses of blood? I can't do anything and I don't want to do anything, because you know, yourself, you, yourself know that a single finger cannot gather flour, you, yourself, know that it's the world that turns, but I, I say that it runs, bro, like you, you ran that morning, why did you run, bro? Why? I ran, too, bro, but not far from my red earth, I ran after you, I ran through the trees, to the water's depths, over the hills, but your face was nowhere on my red earth. You ran like the Earth. To your loss. What do you want me to do with your cash when it's you who ran too far? When everything's lost here? No, bro, I won't do anything. It's easy to run off and demand that others remake the world. I don't care about the world that runs to its loss. You know that! Right, bro?

You know that it wasn't so crazy

You know that we were full of ears, eager ears

You know that that morning a wind swallowed our silence. One morning, Heaven sent us a furious wind that uprooted our silences and now it's impossible to hear the sun's laughter in the morning. No way of cleaning your skin in the dew the morning after the rain drenched the grass, the plants, and the trees. The dew is dead, and it took away our eyes, our laughter, our pulse

You, yourself know that now we've buried all that. On behalf of the government like they said. Today, it's "Hello! Hello! Ciao! Ciao! Yes, hello! Hello! Kiss! Kiss! I can't hear very well! Speak louder, there are too many mopeds, too many cars, shit, I have no more credit, it's going to cut out, where are you? Shit, shit, leave a message. Talk to you soon! I have to leave you, I have to catch the bus, good-bye, talk to you soon, can you call me back later? I'm at the office, call back tomorrow . . ." And all that on behalf of the government as they said. On behalf of the government our childhood began to fall like a rotten mango in the Wèla

You know that the elderly no longer know how to shut up

You know that women no longer know how to listen to their kids

You know that the youth have no more authority

You know that on behalf of the government all around us suddenly 100 years was shoved in our face

What do you want me to do when everything is in a parentheses of blood

I'm tired of this government that robs us of everything and sells us everything in the name of a supposed modernity. What is the point of all these noises that lodge a cough in the air's throat? What is the point of the funerals for the dew when with it, we would hear our pulse, our laughter?

Can you tell me, bro, which sun points its nose towards the horizon? The one that chases after the downfall of our souls? The one of eternal nights? The one that will send us more machines to sweep our houses, our dead, because the Earth is eroding and there's room needed for other things than our laughter; our looks, our grass and its dew? What sun will rise and bring with it that brother who left forever and leaves you a letter telling you, "It's completely magnificent all these bridges, these paved streets, these satellites, these TVs, these Coca-Cola signs, all this civilization, it's all bizarre and seriously fucked. Here are millions of envelopes full of millions of liters of my sweat. Take them and follow the madness of these machines." Will it be a sun for people arriving from nowhere, who pop up everywhere and demolish our souls? A sun of letters? A sun of sweat, of cellphones, of TV? A sun you need to purchase sunlight from, or water? A sun that'll make women's skin wither? Will it be a sun with water that imprisons flesh in flesh? Is water clean when we aren't dirty?

Whichever sun points its nose, I'm telling you, I don't care. Let dogs keep barking! Let people agree at once to everything and to nothing! Let brothers get the hell out and starve as a result, I don't care.

What I'm looking for is an earth

Red earth

Red earth with lots of leaves that cure malaria

I'm looking for a face

A face in which I will see the wounds of my red earth

I'm looking for grass with lots of dew

Grass where I will watch my brother looking at the naked girls

Me, I'm waiting

I'm waiting for the rain

A rain that will dampen my red earth to drive out disease and dust

I'm looking for a baobab where I can lean, exhausted, while waiting for the rain on my red earth

I want to lean, exhausted, on a tamarind tree and laugh at my fucking government and its fucking machines and its shitty fucking development

I want to lean on a mahogany tree and scream into your face everything that I reject, I reject, I reject

I reject TVs

I reject cell phones

I reject Coca-Cola

I reject Chinese rice

I reject fancy rice

I reject GMOs

I reject McDonald's

I reject black plastic bags on my roads

I reject homelessness in my streets

I reject destroyed families

I reject the lack of hospitals

I reject the lack of medications

I reject schools that cost too much

I reject neglected universities

I reject power outages

I reject water shortages

I reject trees cut down

I reject highways

I reject polluted skies

I reject polluted land

I reject polluted seas

I reject privatized factories

I reject dispossessed countryfolk

I reject sold land

I reject sold cocoa

I reject, I reject, I reject, and I reject, bro

Leave me alone with your schools and your hospitals and your bits of lungs and your trickles of blood. Leave me the fuck alone with your delirium. Don't come home, bro. Stay in Paris. Listen to the metro hiss. Drink your beers and keep watching soccer and leave me alone. Don't come. Don't come because here, there's nothing else. Stay in Paris, bro. In Paris, everything is possible, like you said, in Paris, there's everything, but here nothing's left. Nothing but the government that keeps selling everything and privatizing everything while drinking champagne and getting laid. Nothing but highways where our fields, our houses, and our graves used to be. Nothing but the 4x4s, the Chinese mopeds that crush everything, nothing but everyone dressed the same, eating the same thing, thinking the same, the same, the same, the same, stay in Paris my brother, because here there's nothing but the European Union that keeps screwing us over with its goddamned cooperation. Nothing but the Swiss who keep laundering the money of our ministers and dictators. Nothing but France and its aids whom no one sees and its never-ending debts and its Peugeots and its Renaults

And the graves that open up

The dogs that bark

The stars that fill the sky

The hens that jump onto the roofs of the houses

The lambs who no longer bleat

The sun that flees behind the trees

The trees that no longer move

The toads that croak

The voices from far off

The laughing moon

Sounds of eating

Silence of children

Bodies collapsing from exhaustion

More steps

Dogs barking, barking, barking

And me running, running, running

And I who can't any more

And I who piss you off, bro

And I who piss off the government and its machines

And I who tell the NGOs to go fuck themselves with their 4x4s

And I who tell the night to come to my aid

And I who tell the dead to wake up

And I who love the dogs barking, barking, barking

Mon tii suugr yè bidéema huunsu maan

Mon tii kabr daa n'ziidarr maan

Mon tii daahan yè kuupèelaa maan

Mon tii paangaa yè wèla maan

Mon tii suugr yè n'zii huusun maan

Mon tii laafi yè n'naan huusun maan

Guèerr yaan, taalèè yaan

Mii guumaan, mii buusuulèè yan . . .

Ways of Loving

Preface to *Ways of Loving*

By Lionelle Edoxi Gnoula and Safourata Kaboré, who played mother and daughter in the 2015 Festival les Francophonies (Limoges) production. Translated by Anna G. R. Miller.

"What I know and Mama doesn't know, is that owning means losing." (*Ways of Loving*)

In 2015, the Acclamations Theatre invited us to take part in the production of this political, poetic play by the writer and director Aristide Tarnagda. As actors, this production offered us a new text to perform, a theatrical challenge, and also a serious responsibility given the depth of its theme. For me, Edoxi, this was my first exposure to the play. What immediately drew me to it was the question of literal left-handedness. It reminded me of my childhood when, very early on, even before I understood what it meant to write, I had to stop writing with my left hand. Yet another constraint on the bodily freedom of a young woman. Today, I am practically ambidextrous because yes, as an adult, I took ownership of what my left hand could do with a pen. That's how, from the start, I felt a closeness to these characters as women on whom Aristide was shining a political light. For me, it is as if left-handed people are like those on the political left and right-handed people are indelibly tied to the multinational corporations that manipulate the world.

In *Ways of Loving*, Tarnagda gives voice to women and presents the transmission from mother to daughter of issues with political importance. The intellectual submission of women. The impact of bigamy. The hypocrisy of those in power when it comes to the average citizen. The perpetual rebranding of slavery for the financial benefit of the colonizer. This is how I came to love the characters Tarnagda led us to embody on stage. It was so rewarding to perform a play that speaks so directly to us as women, that reflects our identities as people of African heritage who also live on the African continent, and that speaks to us because we are mothers, aunts, sisters, and because our private lives are so tightly tied to national politics. To have is to lose, today's geopolitics remind us of this fact. Today, the weak refuse to claim what is theirs, even while the powerful feel like they are being robbed. Aristide Tarnagda's writing is truly universal.

As for me, Safoura, I had already read *Ways of Loving*. I see the play as inviting consideration of private spaces as ones in which to interrogate our society, politics, choices, the place and freedom of women in society and of Africans in the world. It speaks to the freedom of us as women in our homes, in how we live our lives. To be left-handed isn't just a choice or a bodily movement. To be left-handed in our society is to have one's desires locked away. For me, this play frees women's voices and interrogates the role of Africans in the world. It looks at transmission of knowledge, the relationship between mother and daughter given that very often we teach our daughters the clichés of societal norms, the fear that our children will make the same mistakes as us, the fear of their uniqueness and of their freedom. The writer addresses something that exists in all societies and that is often not spoken about: incest. And the mother's relationship with her father, how many women have had these experiences? As an actor, it is a pleasure to speak the words of the play. It is rare that in one play, a writer successfully captures our pains, frustration, and ways of doing things with words that move us, that heal us, and that, without accusation, poetically interrogate society. Performing this play is a joyful experience as it brings with it palpable engagement from the audience, and it is always fun to be able to incorporate some local vernacular into productions as well.

Enjoy the read and, to those who bring this play to life on stage, enjoy the adventure.

4 Lionelle Edoxi Gnoula and Safourata Kaboré in *Façons d'aimer* (*Ways of Loving*), directed by Aristide Tarnagda in 2015 at the Festival les Francophonies in Limoges, France. Photo © Christophe Péan.

Ways of Loving

Translated by Heather Jeanne Denyer

Ways of Loving presents a young woman speaking her truth to a judge and jury as she stands trial for murder. In this memory play, the woman revisits her complicated relationship with her mother and her experiences as a left-hander, a social outcast, which led her to this day when she stands trial for murdering her husband and his fifth wife–a white woman. The play was developed in residence at the Théâtre National de Bretagne in 2007. It had a reading at the Avignon Theatre Festival in 2013 before its 2015 premiere at the Festival les Francophonies in Limoges, France. It has also been produced in Cotonou, Benin and in Bobo Dioulassou and Ouagadougou, Burkina Faso. The original French version (*Façons d'aimer*) was published alongside *Terre Rouge* by Lansman Editeurs in 2017. It won ADELF's 2018 *Grand prix littéraire d'Afrique noire* (Best African Literary Work, awarded by the French-Language Writers' Association). This translation had a reading in New York as part of the 2018 PEN World Voices Festival. The play has four characters: two women and two men.

Notes on the Translation: This play is written as a monologue; however, it has also been performed with two performers in the roles of Daughter and Mama, and with a third reading for Papa and Husband. The monologue formatting has been kept with dialogue from the past indented twice and dialogue in the present indented once to distinguish them. Additionally, in the original French, ellipses are used to indicate interruptions as well as trailing off and transitions between past and present. For clarity, en dashes have been used in instances where one character is interrupted by another. The dedications in italics were written by the playwright.

Characters

Daughter
Mama
Papa
Husband

To Adama, my grandmother

To my mother

To Assita Souabou

To Mandela Tarndagda

To my sisters Afiatou, Geneviève, Rabi, Aoulatou, Marguerite

. . . Allow me, Mr. Prosecutor, allow me to go look at the Boulgou for the last time, for the last time, I want to see the wind caress that hill over there, I just need to hear the breath of the sun, to savor the smile of the dove who flies through the womb of the Boulgou, I just want to be face to face with the dove, for once there's something I want, even though I've never wanted anything, for once I dare to dream, so don't keep me from that, I will speak, but I won't speak the truth because I don't know what it is, I don't know my right hand. I know, I know, I know, Mr. Prosecutor, I learned that being left-handed was pretty bad, Mama taught me that left isn't good, she even cut the fingers of my left hand with razor blades and slathered them with chili to keep me from using them, but I couldn't leave it alone, my bitch of a left hand, and Mama ended up spilling tears and me, too, because I, I understood Mama's eyes, believe me, Mister Prosecutor, when the chili started, Mama's eyes didn't tell me anything, but when she bared herself for the first time in front of Papa and me, when we saw her completely naked memory, I couldn't hold back my eyes, and I did everything to know my right hand, but I never saw it, so don't ask me to raise my right hand and to tell the truth, nothing but the truth. I never had a right hand, Mama maybe brought me into this world with one hand only, Mister Prosecutor, Papa thinks that Mama kept my right hand between her thighs, but perhaps you will be able to get it back for me, my damned right hand trapped between Mama's thighs, so, Mister Prosecutor, don't ask me to tell you anything at all. And yet there's something I want to say to you, there's something I've always wanted to say, to tell the sea to come to us so people don't leave to go see her and leave you with the memory of your mother, to tell the wind to take me with him when he wanders in the baobab treetops, to tell the shooting star to fly me with her to join the other stars, I want to say something, but not the truth, your truth. I would like to say something, but I won't raise my right hand, you already know why, so if it pleases you, we will break with that tradition, I'm going to say something without yesterday's bullshit, because with yesterday they're always singing the same song, with yesterday's drunk face they always tell you about their experiences, their point of view above all, the way you're supposed to live, where you're supposed to go or not go, whom you should sleep with, with yesterday they controlled you, they formatted you, that's why the memory of Mama forced chili powder on my fingers and told me to not get married because it was polygamy, I already told you, I don't understand all that, maybe there's not even anything to understand, because there's nothing to understand with girls like me, at least that's what Papa said to Mama before Mama's memory forced her to leave, Papa couldn't deal with Mama anymore, he couldn't take the nakedness of Mama's memory anymore, he didn't understand why Mama forced chili powder on the fingers of my left hand, Papa said to Mama:

> What's that supposed to mean what you're doing to her? What sort of witchcraft is that? Don't you understand that we can't all be right-handers?
>
> No, I don't understand, I don't accept that my daughter is left-handed ... You don't care do you? I know that you don't care but let me take care of my daughter, I want to give her a good education, don't get involved in what doesn't concern you—
>
> Yes, it does concern me, for once it concerns me because it's my daughter too, and I'm not going to let you ruin her life—
>
> No! I'm not leaving her life to chance, I want what's good for her. You, you don't care, you're never here, you spend your time playing checkers, getting shit-faced and screwing little girls, those little uneducated left-handers, and you want me to abandon her like those little left-handers, so that you can screw her next, but I won't let you—
>
> I'm going out, I'm leaving, I need to get the hell out of here or else—
>
> Or else you'll do what? Huh! What else do you know outside of getting shit-faced and screwing little left-handers like your own daughter?

No, Mr. Prosecutor, Papa never touched me, I don't know where Mama would have gotten such ideas, but Papa never looked at me, even for a single second, he wasn't the type to look at his daughter, Papa, at least not with the eyes that Mama was talking about, Papa didn't have time to look at anybody, he calmly drank his beer, and he went out to play checkers and that's it. No, Mr. Prosecutor, my father was sweet and me, I loved him, and I think that he did too, only as I told you, it's no longer about understanding us, but to say, to say something, even if there's nothing known, even if there's nothing to say, to say that his daughter was touched, even if all that was done was to calmly drink beer and play checkers, you have to say something to be right, to feed the media, to prove that you are someone, that you love. But Mr. Prosecutor, I am neither against, nor for, I just want you to allow me to look for one moment at that hill across from us, I just need one moment to hear the joy of the dove who meanders over the Boulgou, I just want to see a shooting star, then I will swear to you on that star, that hill, that fig tree, that I will return to the courtroom, I'll come back to tell you something even if I have nothing to tell you, I will try to find my right hand that I left between my mother's thighs and I will lift it up and your damned hearing will begin, I will plead guilty because I killed them, then you will pronounce your verdict, I will respect your verdict even if I know in advance that it will be shitty, and I will go to my cell bare naked like Mama's memory, eyes closed, fists closed, I'll hear nothing more, I'll see nothing more, I'll never say anything ever again, and I'll never leave again, not from the visiting room, no, Mr. Prosecutor, I want to remain condemned, because that's the reality of this century, I accept it, I accept the reality, your reality, the reality of reason, the reality of the deal, of the reckoning, of the twisted logic, the reality of being nothing at all, the reality of being like you to be something, the reality of fleeing, the sad reality of condemnation, of competition, the reality of being a machine under control twenty-four seven. Yes, Mr. Prosecutor, I assure you that I won't run away from your reality. Before, I despised it. But now, I accept it, not because I'm renouncing my reality, but because I have Mama's experience in my ears. Now that I have killed them both, I understand Papa . . .

> I forbid you from thinking, from lying, from saying that I screwed my own daughter. You said it yourself, I'm nothing but a drunk, a checkers player, so leave me to my alcohol and to my board game; or else I promise that you will regret it. I have always allowed you to say anything to me, to insult me as if I wasn't your husband, as if it wasn't I who allowed you to give birth to that poor left-hander that you martyred with your chili powder—

> And me I forbid you to say that I martyred her! I don't want my daughter to be left-handed and it's because I love her that I put chili powder on her fingers. You, you don't love her, you don't understand anything, you don't know what a left-hander is, no, you don't love her, you love your bottles and your game pieces and her little left-handed ass—

> Stop saying that, I'm telling you—

> No, I won't stop, I'll even go to the police if you don't stop.

> You're going where?

> To the police!

> And what are you going to tell them?

> That you don't take care of your daughter.

In my opinion, you'd better go to social services, not to the police because the police don't deal with such things. The police pursue criminals.

That's why I'll go to the police, because a father, a so-called father like you who doesn't worry that his daughter is a left-hander, that she trolls the streets every night with her left hand, with the whore trash in her purse, is a criminal, that type of father is nothing but a criminal who is happy that his daughter is left-handed because he likes to screw the little left-handed girls, you want her to remain left-handed, you did everything so that she looked like me, so that she went after you . . .

I ask myself if there isn't some demon who pushed me to sleep with you, to dare to live all this time with you. But whatever the monster, I'm going to fuck you all, because I, I'm like that, but I don't let myself get upset by bitches like you. Go see whomever you want, tell them whatever you want, I don't care. But if I ever, if I ever hear from the mouth of whomever it may be that you had thought, that you had even insinuated that I had screwed my own daughter because in bringing her into the world you stole her right hand and now you're messing with her, if I ever again hear my daughter let out one single cry because you force chili powder on her fingers, I will come back, I swear to you I'll come back, I'll put down the alcohol, I'll put down the game pieces, I'll trample laws underfoot, and I swear to you on the head of the left-hander that I love, I don't even know why I love her, seeing as how here no one loves left-handers, no more than I know why I love you when you force chili powder on the fingers of our daughter, I don't know why I don't ask for a divorce since you suspect me of cheating on you with my own daughter, even though I've never slept with another, when I am happy simply drinking my beer and moving my game pieces, and that now I'm going to have to leave all that and get the hell out, if not I'll always hear that I screwed the left-hander, my daughter and that will drive me to come back, I'll hear the police bang on my door, and before the police enter, before I open the door to the cops, because I'm going to open the door to them so they can survey the scene, pick up your body, find my DNA all over your blood, on your body splayed out like a pile of shit, your face in pieces, I'm going to give them my hands for the handcuffs, without saying a word, because talking to the cops doesn't do anything when you're an exile, a fugitive, it doesn't do anything to say one single word to the cops, they don't want to understand anything, they only want to know if you premeditated the crime, they only want to throw you in jail, without understanding that the lady who had your DNA in her mouth, on her face, in her blood, they don't know that you loved the lady's body, that you even had a pretty little left-handed girl that you loved, they don't understand, the cops, that left-handers are like Africans, no one wants to look at them, house them, accept them, and so they push back, they react, and that's what the cops don't understand, they don't get that Blacks react, that now the lady is rid of you and you rid of her, and that you, you swear that you love her despite everything, but here the cops are not made to understand, the law isn't made to understand, cops and laws are just assholes made to throw us in jail, that's it, then once in jail without you or the left-hander, I swear to you, I swear to you that I'll drink beer and I'll move my game pieces, and I don't care about anything else . . . And you're going to shut up, for once shut your trap, just be quiet, I beg you, don't do anything at all, please, don't say anything because if you say something, I'll be in jail and you in the cemetery and the left-hander a shadow without memory and all that will be dumb.

Do you think you're intimidating me with your madness? You're mistaken if you think I'm afraid of you, that I'm going to shut up because you've raised your voice, because you're yelling, you think that having balls, means prattling on, means planting left-handers in girls' wombs to be able to screw them later, when they're like Africans and no one needs them, you think that's what being a man is? I won't be quiet, as long as you won't take care of her, as long as you keep her in her left-handed state to be able to screw her, I'll go to the police and I'll tell them everything, and you won't have the time to kill me because the police will already be here to collect you. They don't let criminals like you hang out for long, or else it would be disastrous for the mothers and daughters.

They're already here, your cops?

Soon.

This is goodbye then?

Where are you going?

I'm getting the hell out.

Where?

I may be dumb enough to screw my left-hander, but not so dumb to tell you where the hell I'm going.

Stay. Don't leave. It's not good to piss off, it's foolish to leave like that, to erase yourself from your own family. I'm begging you don't run off, I don't want parts of you! I want you whole, with your game pieces and your beer bottles, I'll leave you in peace with my stories of cops, if you have to get the hell out, I'll forget the police, I'll shove the laws and the police up my ass, now that you want to piss off, I detest them all—

Too late.

I'm telling you that I didn't go to see anyone, I don't even know where the police station is, I only wanted to know if you loved your family, I didn't understand why you never worried that our daughter is left-handed, even though everyone hates left-handers, no man wants a left-hander, because left-handers, they speak too much, they rebel all the time, and you know too well that you men, you don't like the girls who don't make it easy, and left-handers don't make it easy, that's why I put chili powder on her fingers, to make her make it easy, for her to at least have a husband. I didn't understand why that didn't worry you that she is left-handed, so I said to myself that must work out for you in some way, it works out for you that she is left-handed, that way you could screw her, because she attracted no other man besides you, when no one else is interested in girls, they turn to their fathers. That's how it is. I know what I'm talking about. That's it. It's not more complicated than that. And I know that that's crazy to think. But what do you expect? It's the age itself that's crazy, it's now in fashion to screw your own daughter, it's the time when all men drool over the asses of their own children. And as a result of seeing all that on TV, of hearing all these stupidities on the radio, you end up going crazy, distrusting all men, even you. You see?

No. It's too late. Men get tired too, you know?

It's never too late.

Too late, I'm telling you. Good-bye . . .

No, I'm telling you it's never too late, for a long time I believed that it was always too late but no, because I met you, you alone accepted to look at me, to call me. Before you, no one had ever called me. However, I had followed Mama's advice. I never screamed when she put the chili powder on my left hand. I was left-handed before I met you. I shook with my left, I ate with my left, I wiped my ass with my left, I kissed only the left cheek. And Mama told me it was impossible, that I was intolerable because of my left hand. Mama said that if no man ever looked at me, never screwed me, despite my lipstick, despite my beauty, despite my many visits to the dance clubs, it's because I'm left-handed. Left-handers are bad luck, they drive men away, Mama would say. She said it's like Blacks. If you reject them, if you don't allow them to come to where Whites live, if they don't have papers even though the tree that made that very paper came from their country, if Blacks are deported, thrown out, rejected, it's not because you don't like them, it's because they are Black. Being Black is being left-handed. It's having forests but no paper.

I'm so beautiful, as Papa would say.

How juicy my butt cheeks are, as Papa would say.

A forest at the midpoint between my thighs, a moon smile, as Papa would say.

But no man would grant me one second of time.

So, I no longer believed what Mama would say. I turned to Papa. And Papa said that being left-handed wasn't the problem, that if Blacks don't have papers while they have plenty of forests, it's because they make it easy, they let themselves be denied, even from one another. Papa said that he loves me despite my being left-handed. Do you understand? For the first time, a man told me that he loves me. A man. Not my father. A man. And me, I didn't know how, the man didn't know how, but since then, since that moment where the man said to the left-hander that he loved her, she saw her tongue slide into the man's mouth, and the man said nothing, did nothing for or against it, the man simply put his mouth in the forest that is the midpoint between the thighs of the left-hander, and the fruits, the leaves of the forest fell at that moment, at the moment when the man told the left-hander that he loved her, the birds flew over the forest situated at the midpoint between my thighs, the two mouths wailed and Mama arrived . . .

So, since then, Mama started to cut my left hand and to force chili powder on it. She didn't say anything anymore seeing as it was too late for her, every day I stank of her man's scent, the fruits of the forest continued to drop, despite the chili powder on my fingers, and me too, I said that it was too late, that it wasn't right that I stole the scent of Mama's man, I said that it was over, that I was done, but I couldn't do anything, it's like that as a left-hander, Mama said that left-handers are like Blacks, it's not because they're not liked that they're denied, it's because they're African, but Papa said it's because they make it easy, in spite of their forests, and me I don't want to make it easy despite Papa who is always in the forest situated at the midpoint between my thighs despite Mama who no longer says anything, I don't want to let you go, seeing as it is not too late, that it is never too late, or else you wouldn't have come today, you wouldn't have said the same thing to me as Papa, my tongue wouldn't have slid inside your mouth, you wouldn't have replaced Papa in the forest situated at the midpoint between my thighs, and you wouldn't have placed another left-hander at the heart of my forest, so you won't go anywhere, because it's your fault, it's your fault if you suspect, yes it's your fault, leave if you want, leave your shitty DNA on my face if that's what you want, but me, I'm telling you you're the guilty one, it's you who gave me a left-hander, who sooner or later would turn to you, seeing as left-handers, they're like Africans, they sell their forests to whoever and then they're only Africans without papers neither seen nor known of, chased, forced to flee, rejected, exiled, they run away like you, and you, you are obligated to undress, to say nothing, like your mother, to know nothing else at all. Leave then, if you're afraid of cops, get the fuck out if you don't want to understand, I, I'm tired of being naked, that no one understands, and that all we think about is fleeing, after having sold the forests and produced left-handers who steal the scent of your man.

Go then, get the hell out, I'm saying to you . . .

Allow me a moment, Mr. Prosecutor, I would like to return to the hill for a moment, I would like to go look at the hill stretched out over there, and right afterwards I'll tell you everything, even if I have nothing to tell you, but I know that Mama is always prying, as soon as I got home she would immediately throw herself into my purse, and she would look for trash, that trash . . .

I'm looking for the trash you always keep in your purse.

What trash, Mama?

Don't play innocent, don't pretend to not know what I'm talking about.

But, Mama . . .

And she would empty my purse, she would dump out all the contents: cigarettes, condoms, lighter, money . . .

What did I do to you? My god, what have I done to deserve this . . .

What's wrong with you, Mama?

What's wrong with me? My god! She's even making fun of me?

No, I—

Shut up! If you open your mouth again I'll fart in it. Is that clear? What didn't I do so that you could be a girl, a real girl like everyone else. I signed you up for school, I always paid for nice uniforms, I always took you to the hair salon, I always told you that a real woman doesn't cook with her left-hand, I spent all my time at your side, as if you were my lover, my husband, all that so that you would be good, so that you would be a good girl, well educated, so that one day a man would marry you, to keep you from trolling the streets like a prostitute, and above all, so that you wouldn't steal his scent from me. But I was wasting my time. You are nothing but a dirty little whore. Who put those thoughts in your head? Why did you wander off? Do you want me to die, is that it? Well I'm going to die, I'm going to die and leave you in peace, leave you to live your bitch's life, that of a dirty little whore who doesn't care about her mother, because you don't love me I'm going to disappear and leave you in peace, leave you to be left-handed and to not interest any man except for my man. And you're going to see what it's like for a woman to not interest any man, not one single man among the millions will look at you, will ask you, even to touch you, and you will know what it is the drought of touch, when no hand will caress the lines of your whore's body, you will understand, when they all end up fucking you and tossing you aside like an orange peel, you will see what it means to fuck your mother over . . . above all don't say anything to me, I don't want to know anything, your dirty little mouth that knows everything, I'm sick of it, leave me in peace, I don't want to know anything, I don't want to hear anything, I don't want to understand anything, get the fuck out right now, that's all . . .

It's difficult to get the fuck out, Mama, difficult to leave you in peace—

Then I will leave you in peace—

No, Mama, don't leave me in peace—

Then leave me in peace—

When you have disappeared from my heart, then I will leave you in peace, but for the moment, you're there, planted there, even if you think I am a dirty little whore, even if you think that I smoke, that I take drugs—

There you have it! As always, it's me who's crazy, it's me who's always hallucinating, your purse is always filled with a whore's trash, and it's me who's crazy?

What here is a whore's trash?

You don't know what here is a whore's trash? That's rich! The whore doesn't know what trash is whorish? I'm going to tell you, me, what's a whore's trash; I will teach a whore what her accessories are . . . Well then, my dear, all these things are a whore's trash . . . I told you to leave me in peace right now. Don't make fun of me, because despite what you believe, I still have my sense of reason.

And she slammed the door in my face, Mr. Prosecutor. And the idea of becoming a prostitute took over. For the first time, I open my packet of cigarettes. For the first time, I lit my lighter. For the first time, I rolled a joint. For the first time, I opened a condom packet. But the whore didn't last long. She left just as quickly. She went to tear open Mama's door. I went home. She was counting a rosary, kneeling before a statue of the Virgin Mary . . .

Mama? I had never before opened my pack of cigarettes. I had never smelt the scent of a condom. The whore never lived in my body. Because you suspected me of coming back every night from the streets, I wanted to know what a cigarette smells like, or a joint, how to put on a condom. Otherwise I just kept them in my purse, to be a lady of the times, as they say, so that people would look at me even if I am left-handed, I tried to identify myself, it's a question of not being too uptight, too wild, too stupid, but the foolishness of a prostitute as you call it never seduced me, but now that you no longer believe me, I wanted to be a whore to feel the disgust that it hides, the stupidity contained, to understand why the whore bothers Mama, why the girl who wants to smoke won't smoke, why the girl who wants to sleep with all the men on Earth won't fuck them all, why we see the devil everywhere even though the sky is blue, why the left-hander saw her left hand hacked with a blade and burned by chili powder, and yet I always called you Mama, I didn't leave, I didn't go to see UNICEF or the media to tell them that Mama put chili powder on my left hand, I didn't even scream to alert the neighbors, I just understood, I just accepted that you were taking care of me, in your own way, that you love me, in your own way, I simply believed you, without seeking to know if Mama was right or not, because I had nothing to do about it, whether you were right to not, whether you were mistaken or not, seeing as everyone is wrong sometimes, we assert ourselves, we set up experiments, as masters, I made it easy, but you, you don't play the game, you don't try to understand me, you just want me to be the way you want me to be and for everyone to sing your praises as an exemplary mother, that you have educated your daughter well, you are alone in your concerns, and I, I have to deal with it.

I'm going to do it, Mama, I'm going to do it, I'm going to do it. For the first and the last time I don't smoke anymore, my purse will be emptied or filled with anything you want, and you'll no longer have to count your rosary, I just want you to check one thing, I just want you to see if something deep in me is still in place, check that it hasn't been touched yet, I want you to check if the orange inside of my orange tree still has its juice, Mama. Wear a condom, Mama, whores have AIDS based on what they say, I don't want to contaminate you, if the whore is encrusted in the orange housed deep inside of me.

Go ahead. And after, I'll kiss you, Mama, and you will see if my saliva has the taste of that of a prostitute.

After your exam, whether I pass or fail, I will run away into the Boulgou and I will watch the dove soaring above the neem trees and the fig trees and I will say nothing ever again, I will forget my left hand and I'll always understand you.

You see, Mr. Prosecutor?

Allow me just one moment to understand, to understand how a beautiful evening when you are across from the hill, that hill on which one beautiful evening he told you that he carried you in him, that right away you told him without asking yourself any questions, without seeking to know if he was sincere or not despite Mama's distrust, because Mama knows that on those hills, in those gardens, in those bars, on the streets, the lie was planted, on that hill two years since I had been with him, since I had shared him with three other women, on that hill then, Mr. Prosecutor, he told me . . .

    I'm packing my bags. I'm taking a flight in a week.

What do you do, Mr. Prosecutor?

Tell me what to do, you who know everything, you who have experience, you who know all the written laws, you who condemn me?

    I'm packing my bags. I'm taking a flight in a week.

Mr. Prosecutor, what do I do?

When the dove disappears, what do I do?

When the sky loses its blue color, what do I do?

When the neem trees and the fig trees turn yellow, what do I do?

Because I am left-handed and being left-handed is being African, Mama says that it's because Africans are Black, people don't like them, it's because they're without papers, but Papa says it's because they sell their forests and they make it easy. Mr. Prosecutor? What do I do now that there are no more forests for the paper? Since the sea isn't here, since there's no wheat here, to be Black is to be African and to be African is to be left-handed, when I left my right hand in my mother's thighs?

Do I play the hypocrite, do I ask him why he went back to the sea? Do I play the abandoned lover and cry out? And beg him to stay?

I play the girl who is happy to see her guy get the hell out and jump on his neck to lie to him that I am proud of him, that I'm happy that he's leaving? Or do I assault him with this type of questions: Why do you want to leave even though we're good together on this hill? You don't love me anymore is that why you're leaving? Is it your family that's making you leave? It's the same over there as here, you know that, right? You're not going to cheat on me over there? Do I play the lost girl because the guy I love is leaving?

What would you do, Mr. Prosecutor, on that hill when the sky loses its color, when the dove disappears, when the fig trees and the neem trees are on strike because they heard:

    I'm packing my bags. I'm taking a flight in a week.

Not even a week, tomorrow, in just a few hours, Mr. Prosecutor, in a few hours only, mister packed his bags . . .

I don't ask him why. I couldn't care less why.

Because I know that in this country, they're all programmed to get the hell out and it's not difficult to understand. You just have to open your eyes and see that here there is no sea, that all the suns have the same face, everyone counts on everyone else even though everyone says to everyone else that they are nothing, because the land has been sold, the sun sold, oil sold, cocoa sold, cotton sold, all the forests desecrated, and so you and I, we are nothing because there it is, it's too easy, it's too stupid, we are African, we are not American, we are not French, we are not Chinese, we are not Palestinian, we are not Japanese, there it is, it's too simple, it's too stupid, Mr. Prosecutor, but it's like that, it's like that, that you sell everything, it's stupid what happened to us but I can't do anything if we were persuaded to sell everything, to convince them that they are nothing and that they have to be American or French or Italian or Canadian to be guys, girls, happy mamas and papas.

So I didn't answer?!

I didn't cry?!

I didn't laugh?!

I listened for a moment to the wind, the sea, the TV, the dreams that, like the waves of a wild sea, were dragged off far away over there?!

I listen to the anger and emptiness around us that kicked him in the butt to make him get the hell out?!

Listened to everything without hearing anything?! Without crying?!

Without laughing?!

No, Mr. Prosecutor, I listened to this emptiness and I understood his need to leave.

Allow me then to go listen and I will come back to tell you something, I promise you that I will come back to tell you something, that which you want to hear, I will tell you that it was I who killed them, the families will cry, I know, everyone will forever loathe me, I know, my co-wives will blame me for having taken their husband away, I know, the defense will go on and on, demonstrating that they are eloquent, I know, I know, I know all that . . . My attorney, no, I don't need one, even if the law says I must, I won't say anything if I have a lawyer, if you want me to give you your truth, that everyone see you on TV like all those left-handers who sold everything and got the hell out, don't stick a lawyer on my ass. So if I don't have a lawyer, I will come back to you in the courtroom in a few moments, trust me, put surveillance cameras all over if you want, put watchdogs all over if you want, elite snipers on all the roofs and trees, do what you want to, as you want to, if like Mama, you don't trust me, after all you have the right to not trust me, to trust in your laws, in your experiences of tracking criminals like me, you have the right to be like Mama, like Mama who said to me:

> I don't understand that way of seeing things, I'm telling you that that way of more than one loving the same man debases a woman to a position of being dominated, a slave of the male, I, I'm telling you, I don't like that way of loving. I don't like my daughter's way of loving, she turned herself into a reproductive apparatus, a machine in which the man she pretends to love comes to her when

> he feels like depositing an egg in the machine and stands there with his arms crossed for nine months waiting for her to push out a baby for him. No, I don't like your way of loving. I'm telling you clearly and openly, but do whatever you want.

Thank you, Mama, but I, I like my way of loving.

> And him does he love you? Are you sure that he loves you? With three other wives, does he have the time to love you?

I don't know, Mama, but I don't care.

> You will see, you will see that I'm right despite everything you believe, despite all the illusions that cloud your eyes. You will see that I'm your mother and that's why I know more than you, I speak to you from experience. You'll see that you will be abandoned like one piece of shit for another. You'll see that time will harass you and, believe me, when time corners us on every side, we don't spoil on the outside; no, we wither on the inside, in our guts, in the most noble part of a woman. And when time has rotted you away from the inside, you'll begin to whine like a bitch harassed by a pack of dogs, except that in your case, these will be other bitches: two, three, four bitches who monopolize your mate, then the more you whine, the more time will rot you from the inside, nice and deep until your guts secrete jealousy, hatred, and welcome the war between the bitches pursuing the same mate, farewell to your way of loving, you will see, you will see my dear that you'll pick up your odds and ends, with a little luck you'll have your face disfigured, your spirit faded, your gleaming eyes, you will see, you'll see my daughter that I, I will be the same when you get back here because mother and daughter are one contagious disease.

So, you have every right, Mr. Prosecutor, like I had the right to not take Mama's advice into consideration, I didn't care about Mama's experience, I didn't care that this man had multiple wives. No, Mr. Prosecutor, because I didn't want to own him. Because, what I know and Mama doesn't know, is that owning means losing. When you own what you love you will lose it, inevitably you will lose it, because no one likes to be owned, even your dog doesn't like to be owned. Otherwise he bites you. He gives you back the rage that you infected him with by owning him, those who own the laws will always be exploited, the rich will always be bitten by the poor, and in the end, there will be chaos, destruction, seeing as the whole world will be owners: you, the laws for condemning; the rich, their bank accounts and weapons for beating down the poor; the Africans, their hatred towards those who dispossessed them of everything; the criminals, their guns; and in the end, there will be shots fired, there will be shots fired everywhere, there will be shots fired towards the end, Mr. Prosecutor, and this will be hell, fucked up because of our possessive insanity, because of our egocentrism, we all want to be at the summit of the Boulgou looking down at the others below us, and that, Mr. Prosecutor, is not pretty, I assure you it's not pretty, that's why I content myself to stay at the bottom of the Boulgou, allow me then one moment to return to the base of the Boulgou, then I will come back to tell you something, just let me go to smile at the dove that skims the flanks of the sky with its wings, let me just see the sun close its eyes, then I will come back to tell you what you want to hear, I will tell you that a few days after his:

I'm packing my bags. I'm leaving in a week.

After the dove has disappeared, after the sky has taken a color other than blue, the fig trees and the neem trees have started their strike, after the sea, the money, the drought, the lack of jobs, the few that own everything, after all that has taken away our men, he left, Mr. Prosecutor.

I didn't kiss him!

I didn't look at him!

I didn't cry!

I didn't laugh!

I didn't accompany him to the airport!

I didn't make love to him!

He didn't screw me!

I didn't say goodbye to him!

It wasn't my turn, but someone else's, the second wife's, each of us had one week, and when it wasn't my week I was at the Boulgou, it's like that when you love the same person, and me, it didn't bother me that they loved the same person as me, because that gave me more people to love, especially since now it's difficult to find people to love, there are no people who love you, because you won't find any, seeing as people all run up to the summit of the hill, towards ownership, people spend their time singing to you:

I want my own house

I want my own car

I want my own bank account

I want my own Boeing

I want my own moon

I want the Goncourt Prize

I want to be French, American, Italian, white, mixed-race

I want my own France

I want Trump's America

I want an Africa attached to my Europe

I want to be Ronaldino or Zidane or Pélé or Maradona

I want to be Bob Marley or Alpha Blondy or Johny Alide

And I want, I want, I want, Mister Prosecutor.

But I didn't want anything that day, when, after five years of absence, he came back. He had returned with a fifth wife, Mr. Prosecutor. He met her over there and it's normal for a woman to meet a man and for a man, if he is already the husband of four women, meeting another woman, to not tell her that he's already taken, as we say here, because she wouldn't understand, wouldn't accept, because she wants to own him and I, I know that even dogs don't accept that, and I'm telling you to leave me the fuck alone, I'm telling you that I'm sick of not being able to leave to just re-join the Boulgou to look at the dove and the shooting star and the fig trees and the neem trees, and I'm telling you that I will not lift my right hand, I can't do anything about it if my right hand stayed trapped in Mama's thighs, leave me the fuck alone I'm telling you, I need to look at something other than your ugly face, I want to go back to the trees, the dogs, the moon that disappears over there, the wind that carries away those we love, the rain that doesn't come here anymore, and everybody who runs, runs, runs towards there where it rains, where the sea is, there where our forests have gone, there where you can become something, there where you own, and I'm fucking with you, Mister Prosecutor, I'm going to kill you, I'm going to beat you like I beat them, her and him, even though I didn't want to touch them, but what do you want, Mr. Prosecutor, when you are left-handed, you're African, and Africans are Blacks as they say, and as they say, Blacks can only do lefty things, whores' trash, Mama's way of speaking, but maybe Mama was right, maybe I am a dirty little whore, I don't know, Mr. Prosecutor, I told you I don't know anything, not even the truth, so what do you want me to tell you, when I have nothing to say, I just want to hear the verdict, that the cell be opened for me, so that completely naked with my left-handed memory, I will go to the window and look out at the Boulgou, the sky, the fig trees, the dove. Everything else, I don't care. After his return, even then I asked nothing of him, not even to fuck me, not even to buy me clothes, not even to look at me, I accepted becoming his cousin, his sister, because the white woman decided that we were all his cousins, his sisters, and I cooked for them for him and his white woman, every morning, every noon, every night, I made their bed, I cleaned the sheets . . . No, Mr. Prosecutor, becoming my husband's cook didn't bother me at all, what bothered me, what bothered my left hand more precisely, was when we crossed paths in the kitchen by accident, him and me, like under the Boulgou, and my mouth moved towards his mouth, I don't know why, my mouth was maybe too dry, you know, Mr. Prosecutor, what that's like, the drought of a mouth? Like the land, my mouth was dry and naturally moved towards his tongue, his tongue that had disappeared for five years from this one, his tongue that had been in the white woman's mouth every day, so my tongue moved towards his mouth to wet itself just a little after five years of thirst, five years during which I had shut down my whole body, exactly, Mr. Prosecutor, exactly like the bodies that you lock up, those bodies that you throw in jail with your stupid laws, but he, he understood nothing, didn't want to understand anything, he pushed me aside like a piece of shit, a big load of shit, he pushed us aside me and my mouth parched for him, even though I had accepted becoming his cousin, I had accepted becoming the servant of his wife, even though I didn't want to own him. So, Mr. Prosecutor, I don't know any more about it, I already told you I know nothing. Condemn me and leave me in peace, because if he hadn't pushed me, if I hadn't had that knife in my hand, if she hadn't by chance come into the kitchen, I don't know anything, Mr. Prosecutor, I won't tell you anything, stick me with the verdict that you like, the verdict that suits criminals of my background, do what you want with me, but leave me in peace.

I don't want anything else.

I just want to go for one moment by the Boulgou.

I just want to go watch the dove caress the sky with its wings. I just want to go see a shooting star.

All the rest, it's a big mess that I don't understand, and Mama was right, it's time that harasses us, and when you have time on your heels, the prosecutor on your ass, your tongue that's drying out and him pushing you away, you are forced to react, like Papa's Blacks, so with the knife in your left hand, all you can do is stab him in the heart, in the throat, that fucking throat that rejected you. Everything else is a mess, Mr. Prosecutor, a mess that your cousin, the white woman infiltrated, the white woman slipped into this mess, and I was forced to send the knife into her heart, I don't know why, I reacted to the mess of the moment and that's it, because despite everything, it's Papa and Mama who were right, not you, Mr. Prosecutor, no, you can't be right, only Mama and Papa are right, these times are messed up and we're rotting away from the inside, only knots in our guts, knots, Mr. Prosecutor, the times are shitty, and Africans are forced to leave, seeing as they were dispossessed of everything and that now they're without forests, without seas, without oil, without land, without cotton. That's everything I know, Mr. Prosecutor, the rest, it's my tongue that knows, it's my knife that knows, these are the witnesses that know.

Interrogate them, Mr. Prosecutor. I will confess everything. I will lift my left hand and I will swear to tell you . . .

Sank, or the Patience of the Dead

Preface to *Sank, or the Patience of the Dead*

By Dr. Fatou Ghislaine Sanou, Professor and Scholar of African Literature at the Université Joseph Ki-Zerbo (Ouagadougou). Translated by Anna G. R. Miller.

Sankara, a Tragedy of the Unfinished

What if we thought of Thomas Sankara as a character in search of an author? An answer to this question already exists since, dear readers, you are holding in your hands a translation of the play *Sank, or the Patience of the Dead* by Aristide Tarnagda. How should the story of this revolutionary of August 1983 be told? The character that this Burkinabè playwright renders is the result of a process of literary mythification of the revolutionary. But just as Pirandello points out in his celebrated play *Six Characters in Search of an Author*: "One doesn't give life to a character for nothing." In the play, the reader sees the character of Sank come back to life, recount the final hours before his assassination, bear witness to his journey, his battles, and his dream of a revolution. The magic of the theatre revives the memory of this man who "dared to invent the future" of his country and his continent, as he famously said, by taking a stand against imperialism. And it cost him his life.

To experience the play is to see in its dialogues an illustration of inexpressibility, the performance of which can only be found in the journey of a man misunderstood during his lifetime. Indeed, over the years, Thomas Sankara's aspirations for liberty and peace have made him a symbol of popular idealism. We can read the character's return to life at the beginning of the play as a demand for recognition of his existence and for uncovering the true circumstances of his death. It is believed that the dead rest in peace if and only if the truth of their disappearance is exposed. In this way, the play offers a vertiginous meditation on the mysteries of the dark hours that continue to haunt millions of his country's citizens and people across the globe. The dominant feeling is thus one of profound unease reflected in the image of a man who does not succeed in realizing his dream of happiness for his people. The relationship between reality and fiction that thus emerges is one that evokes a certain *tragedy of the unfinished*. In writing this play on the history of his country, Tarnagda seems to announce that artistic creation does indeed draw its inspiration from life as we know it and yet also belongs to a reality whose truth sometimes remains incomprehensible.

Today, we know the man to be an immortal hero. Thousands of people across his country and the world grieve the loss of Thomas Sankara. Admiration intensifies this grief. This is the mark of a hero. His speeches and his writings, as much as the work he began, are still remembered by generations of youth who see themselves as committed to the fight against imperialism and injustice. It remains true that the fundamental stakes of the theatre are ones of encounter, transmission, and sharing. Perhaps as a response to the vital need to experience our national historical figures, Aristide Tarnagda created a series of shows about Joseph Ki-Zerbo, Norbert Zongo, and Thomas Sankara. This has allowed audiences to (re)discover voices that echo the realities of Sankara's time and, crucially, of our own.

Sankara's battlecry still sounds: "Homeland or death, we will win!"

Is Thomas Sankara resting in peace after the 2021–2 trial for his murder and that of his officials present that day, the life sentence handed down to the primary suspects Blaise Compaoré and Gilbert Diendéré, and the subsequent burial of his exhumed remains at the site of the crime? Waiting more than thirty years for progress toward what could be considered the end of this legal slog has rekindled some tensions around the symbolism of returning to the crime scene. One woman has fought for an end to this waiting: his wife Mariam. October 15, 2023, marked the 36th anniversary of the tragedy. On this day, a commemoration ceremony was held at the Thomas Sankara Memorial in Ouagadougou, where the father of the Revolution and his camarades rest forevermore. One could even call this play, "Mariam, or the Patience of the Living." "The country has had enough of your time. Now, it's our time, time for your family, time for your children, for your wife ..." as she says in the play. In spite of everything, the revolutionary leader pursues his work for the honor of his country. The response comes quickly: "I, I defy death so that the reign of fools may dawn!"

His mad pursuit of justice haunts him day and sleepless night. It is thus clear that "sleep does not govern," as the African proverb teaches us. Tarnagda's writing reveals itself at the heart of this unfinished human work—thus marked with the stamp of imperfection—that the people call a "shooting star" in the play. And to be sure, whispers of hope remain. "Let's hope that after this star, a people's people will topple the throne of the imperialist people."

Dear readers, you hold in your hands an edifying piece of theatre: it forces us to look, to sharpen our attention on humanity, to decode our society, and to interrogate systems of value. Hence the fundamentally political and enlightening qualities of Tarnagda's theatre.

5 David Malgoubri, Alain Hema, and Alberto Martinez Guinaldo in *Sank, ou la patience des morts* (*Sank, or the Patience of the Dead*), codirected by Aristide Tarnagda and Pierre Lambotte in 2016 at the Théâtre de la Guimbarde (Belgium) in collaboration with the Théâtre Eclair (Burkina Faso). Photo © Valérie Burton.

Sank, or the Patience of the Dead

Translated by Heather Jeanne Denyer

Sank, or the Patience of the Dead takes on the final moments of the life of Thomas Sankara, the Marxist revolutionary leader from 1983 to 1987 of the independent country that he renamed Burkina Faso—land of the upright people. The play brings Sankara back to life to portray intimate glimpses of his final battles, those with his wife and with Blaise Compaoré, the brother in arms who would betray him and assume the presidency in his stead. In 2016, the play had a reading at the Avignon Theatre Festival and premiered at the Palais des Beaux Arts in Belgium. It was also performed at the Tropiques Atrium Theatre in Martinique in 2019. The original French version (*Sank, ou la patience des morts*) was published by Lansman Editeurs in 2016. The play has nine characters: six men and three women. The People may be played by actors other than those playing Sank, Blaise, and Mariam.

Characters

The People
Sank
Blaise
Mariam
Mother
Lion
Chantou
Banker
Gilbert
Pen

"Have faith in your dreams, for it is in them that the gateway to eternity hides."

The prophet Khalil Gibran

It's the hour where the sun says goodbye to the small city dams of Ouagadougou. Car motors whir. Bicycles click and clack. Red dust and the smoke escaping exhaust pipes continue their dizzying ascents.

Suddenly, the voice of Thomas Sankara overcomes the brouhaha of the city.

Sank (*heard from offstage*)   Don't worry. It's me they're looking for.

The voice is killed by shotgun fire. Bodies crumble. Blood runs. Vultures circle the sky that is red with dust and black with smoke escaping from exhaust pipes.

Scene One: The murmurs of the people

− It's over. They got him.
− We are screwed. Those hyenas always take our honest men. He warned us: If Burkina Faso refuses to pay the debt itself, I won't be here for the next summit. Go in peace, Captain. Go. This country doesn't deserve you.
− I think he came too soon. People weren't ready.
− Remember what he said: You can't kill an idea. He left us with ideas. It's up to us to realize them.
− So that they kill us all? You think those people are fooling around?
− It's dark thoughts like those that are the real mortal bullets that will put the guy in his grave. How could they kill all of us?
− That'd be nothing! They could raze all of Africa if they wanted to, in the blink of an eye. It's not difficult: two atomic bombs and it's over—we're over.
− I told everyone here that those whites over there weren't going to let him keep going.
− Hey, brother, leave the whites where they are. The whites didn't do anything. This guy isn't the first to be killed by his own brothers: Lumumba, same thing: it was the Congolese—
− Wrong; totally wrong. The Congolese simply executed orders from the Americans and the Belgians . . . Everyone knows that as soon as there is a real African leader who wants to take his country out of shit, the westerners will do anything to get him killed . . .

Scene Two: The beginning of the end

A body emerges from the dead bodies. It's **Sank**. *He sits down on a chair and starts to write frenetically.* **Blaise**, *like a ghost, prowls around him.* **Mariam** *emerges from the bedroom and sees her husband still writing. Exasperated, she goes back to bed. The murmurs of people begin again.*

– It began with Samori Touré, Ahmed Sekou Touré, Nelson Mandela, Patrice Lumumba, Kwamé Nkruma . . .

– Rosa Luxembourg, Jean Jaurés, Julien Lahaut . . . Have we ever seen a Westerner shoot an African leader? It's always a Negro who fires the gun . . . You have to stop always looking for a scapegoat. The Whites, the Whites. I'm sure that behind those gunshots the crocodiles of Yamoussoukro are hiding with the hyenas from Lomé and even the hawks from Libreville . . .

– It's started again . . . Fuck that pisses me off . . . The guy gave himself up for nothing . . . Look, more people have internalized the dominant discourse: they think that African people are nothing more than savages killing each other . . .

– It's western bankers who manipulate everything. For those people, we don't count. We have nothing to say; we have no history; we have no path, no sky, no land, no soul; we are a misery for the world that they can't tolerate . . .

– That's the truth, Brother—

– Right, the truth, my ass!

– If we know those people don't like us, why do we keep cooperating with them? Why do we keep welcoming them to our palaces as advisors? Why do we keep killing our blood brothers for people we know don't like us?

Sank My only ambition is a twofold aspiration: First, to be able to speak in plain language in the name of my people, the people of Burkina Faso, where millions of children, women, and men refuse to die of ignorance, of hunger, and of thirst.

Second, to be able to express in my own way the word of the people, of the underprivileged of the world. A world where humanity has been transformed into a circus, destroyed by the fighting between great and not-as-great powers, beaten by armed groups, subjected to violence and to pillaging. To tell them—even if I don't succeed in making them understand—the reasons why we are revolting.

I want to make it clear that we feel on our cheek every single blow issued to every person in the world.

It is essential, it is urgent that our elected officials learn there is no such thing as harmless writing. In these tempestuous times, we cannot leave the monopoly of thought, imagination, and creativity to our enemies of yesterday and today.

If the source of all our woes is politics, then the cure must be political.

So, let us choose to risk new paths to be happier. Let us learn to simply live.

Let us reject the surveillance state; let us free our campaigns from regressing to a medieval immobility; let us truly democratize our societies; let us open our spirits to a universe of collective responsibility to dare to invent the future.

Let us answer the cruel threat of drought by planting trees and by creating a communal fund. Let us expand the public health care.

Allow yourselves to listen to me when I say:

I speak in the name of the millions who are in the ghettos because they have black skin or they're from different cultures, who have a status barely higher than that of an animal.

I speak in the name of the unemployed, reduced to only seeing in life the reflections of the lives of the rich.

Mariam *appears in a nightgown and pleads with* **Sank**.

Mariam Thomas!

Sank (*still writing*) I speak in the name of the women around the world who suffer from a system of exploitation imposed by men. Women today need to be represented in all levels of government and social life in every country in the world.

Mariam Thomas!

Sank Women need to fight and to declare that the slave incapable of accepting to revolt does not deserve pity for their lot.

Mariam It's 2 a.m., Thomas. Soon the rooster calls mixed with those of the muezzins, and the sounds of housekeepers' brooms mixed with mopeds will invite all to work.

Sank Sorry, Mariam. I'm almost done. I'll be with you in a minute.

Mariam Thomas, this is too much! At this pace I'll soon be a widow and this house an orphanage . . .

Sank Don't worry. Above all, I am military! I've lived through worse, and I never got sick.

Mariam Thomas, do you know how long it's been since your scent was on our sheets?

Sank Ah! The missus is actually pursuing her own interests! But she shouldn't worry. She'll get her time after our pains are birthed on paper . . .

Mariam, *hopeless, goes back to bed and* **Sank** *starts to write frenetically again.*

Sank I speak in the name of the deprived mothers of our countries who see their children die of malaria or dysentery, ignorant that there are simple ways to save them that the multinational enterprises don't offer, preferring to invest in cosmetic laboratories and in plastic surgery to serve the whims of a few women or men whose vanity is threatened by the excessive calories from their overly rich meals, and so often making you—no, more like making us, the others in the Sahel—dizzy. These simple means, let's adopt them and make them widespread.

Sank's **Mother** *enters.*

Mother Thomas

Sank Coming, Mariam. Just a minute . . .

I'm also speaking of the child. The poor child who is hungry, and who sneaks towards the accumulated abundance of the rich-people's boutique. The boutique protected by a thick window. The window protected by an impenetrable grill. And the grill guarded by a helmeted police officer, masked, and armed with a truncheon.

Mother Isidore!

Sank Mom?

Mother My tongue came here to register, to confide to your ears that my nights, the nights of your father, and those of your brothers and sisters are long. All our nights are interminable, full of black and white dogs who never stop chasing you. Isidore, my son, these nights full of black and white dogs can only forecast days drunk with tears. So, I have come to register, to confide in your ears, words from your father and from me as well. I told your father to come with me so that together we could put your stubbornness on notice, but he didn't want to. He said: "You know your son well. As stubborn as he is, you can't find anywhere else on this Earth." He was satisfied to tell me: "Go, if you want to, tell him that if he still has time for his father, then he can come see me. But I won't go there."

"In any case, if you had listened to me, we wouldn't be here today. I told you that Thomas in politics was not a good thing. You didn't listen to me." I said that to your father. But for fathers, it's always this way. Incapable of foreseeing the mistakes, the losses, the suffering of their children. Believing that they have no connection with their children. Because I knew that politics is not for honest people. I knew that. But your father didn't listen to me. As always. Men never listen to their wives. The day they listen to their wives, this world will finally and forever escape from these interminable nights. But in waiting, you are my son, and you will listen to me: I didn't bring you into this world for the world. Do you understand? You are not the child of the world. When I defied the aridness of the ground so that your stomach never went empty; when every night, in secret, I begged the stars to not let meningitis, or dysentery, or any other disease that we don't have treatments or vaccination for plunge you and me and your brothers and sisters into nights without them, the stars, the world; he drank his beers and danced in nightclubs. So, stop mixing in the affairs of the world and come answer your father's call, your family's. Stop speaking, Thomas, you say too much.

People everywhere whisper that you are attacking the important people in the world, and that soon your smart little mouth is going to be shut . . .

Scene Three: Heresy

Sankara *is writing his debt speech.*

Sank I believe that debt should first be assessed according to its origin. The origins of debt can be traced back to colonization. Those who lent us money are those who colonized us. It's the same people who controlled our economies. It's the colonizers who indebted Africa to lenders: their brothers and cousins. We are strangers to debt. So, we can't pay it.

We're told to pay back the debt. It's not a moral question. It's no longer a question of so-called honor to repay or not to repay. First of all, the debt can't be repaid because, if we don't pay it, our lenders won't die. Let's be clear about that. On the other hand, if we pay it, it's we who are going to die. Let's be clear about that, too. Those who drove us to indebtedness were playing a game. As long as they were winning, there was no problem. Now that they're losing, they're demanding that we pay back the debt. And they speak of a crisis. No, Mister President: they played; they lost; those are the rules of the game. And life goes on!

We can't pay back the debt because we're not responsible for it. On the contrary, we can't pay back the debt because others owe us something that the greatest riches can never pay for, which is the blood debt. It's our blood that was spilt . . .

Noises from the street.

– Hey, Sankara! San-ka-ra! There's a real boy. Finally, an African who is trying to speak the truth to those assholes from IMF and the World Bank. A beer for everyone to celebrate the African renaissance!

– You talk about a renaissance? Let's get the coffins ready, instead!

– It's another Afro-pessimist!

– I'm an Afro-realist. That guy is definitely toast.

– Fuck, what is this speech?

– Is he crazy or what? Even a crazy person wouldn't be this crazy!

– He's said out loud what other presidents say to themselves.

– And he'll be hanged straight off while the others, perched on high, continue to profit off the state.

– After delivering such a speech to the world you become immortal.

– That's what we'll see. May God give us long enough life. Amen.

Scene Four: Conspiration

African Unit at the Elysée, Paris.

Banker That's where a lack of balls gets us. In Christ's name, what the fuck are you doing? It's been four years that you've let that Negro brat take himself too seriously, and the Negro, you can't ever, ever, ever let him take himself too seriously. If not, well, there he is, thinking he's cleverer than you. There he is: having just stepped out from his vines and baobab trees; he takes himself for Marx or Hegel. There he is teaching you the law, justice, freedom, *patati, patata* . . .

Scene Four: Conspiration

Ah, the Negro. It's funny, isn't it? We should be careful to not wipe out all of their forests; that way, there will still be authentic ones, and we can—us and our Negro allies who have evolved a little—continue to enjoy ourselves a bit. . . . But while we wait, Mister Politician, we don't want our orders not to be respected. You were given the order to not allow that Negro son of a bitch to believe himself to be more kingly than the king. What the fuck have you done? Do you need to be reminded that you are not the head of state to reflect or to make decisions? You are employed for our business, and when we tell you to do this to the letter, it should be done properly. That's the contract that binds us, Mister Politician. Don't act like the Negros. Don't confuse illusion for freedom, the illusion of power for power. No, it's not the same, Mister Politician. You are an actor, period. And you're paid to play this role. So, this is the last time we're going to tell you: We can't let ourselves be humiliated by these Negro assholes that we plucked from the forest. Not satisfied with refusing to thank us, they mock us. And you know, the Negro is contagious. Just from the smell. And if we leave this little Negro alone for any longer, he's not only going to stink up all of Africa with his stench of Communist shit, he'll finish by contaminating your own people. Then hello damages. There we would be, fighting on multiple battlefronts because we didn't exterminate the rats in the one corner in time. So do us the honor of cleaning up that corner. His requiem mass should be spoken in front of the next gathering of Negros. And do it in a way that he serves as an example for all the other Negros who wanted to take themselves too seriously. Fear, man, these Negros need to feel fear. If we are in deep shit today with their fucking independence, it's because we put off instilling fear. And if this monkey, barely out of his monkey diapers, mocks us this badly, that means that there's no fear on their side, and without fear, man, no business. They have to be afraid, the Negros. Fear in their bones, fear in their guts, fear in their minds, fear in their dicks, fear in their trees, fear of us. From now on, we'll keep our TVs on for any updates. It's in all our interests. Goodnight.

They leave.

Home of **Blaise**. **Chantou** *is packing.*

Blaise   Where are you going?

Chantou   I'm going back home.

Blaise   Why?

Chantou   I'm tired of living like a beggar. I am not a maid.

Blaise   Why are you saying that?

Chantou Are you kidding me?

Blaise What do you mean?

Chantou Okay. When you have realized why . . .

Blaise Stop, honey . . .

Chantou Don't touch me! You do not touch me. Is that clear? . . . Is it clear? . . .

Blaise It's clear . . .

Chantou And that "honey," that has to stop right now, okay? Honey, honey, take that honey out from your mouth. It's not you, whoa, it's my father who got me into this mess . . .

Blaise Will you just tell me what happened?

Chantou Ohhhhh! God! My coco doesn't know what's going on. The poor thing! Look how lost my poor coco is. God forgive me, but I'm going to bring my coco up to speed: what's going on, my coco, is that I, Chantou, whom you see right here, I am tired of living like a peasant. I am tired of living like a maid. That's it. You know, yourself. Or else? What's going on? You're real funny! What's going on . . . What's going on, my coco, is that I'm not spending one more day in this barn that serves as your house. No champagne in the fridge, no air conditioner in your damn barn, I, Chantou, am suffocating. What's going on is that I'm not eating any more shit from your dusty shelves. Your "handwoven textile-thingy," I, Chantou, can't take any more. You get it now, my coco, or do you need me to paint a picture for you?

Blaise But, what don't you understand, hon— . . . Is this my fault? We're in a revolution and the revolution means sacrifices, hon— . . .

Chantou Fine! As I, Chantou, am not revolting, I'm going back home. What's the problem? When you've finished your revolution, let me know.

Blaise Please, try to understand me . . .

Chantou But I do understand you, my coco. You're revolting. But you also need to understand Chantou. Chantou isn't made to live in a barn and to sleep like sardines in a can. No, no, no. Chantou is well-born, and for the souls of the well-born, you know the rest, my coco. My father always told me: if your husband doesn't have more than your father, go back to your father. Have a good revolution, my coco.

Scene Four: Conspiration

Blaise   You want expensive champagne?

Chantou   You've known that from this first.

Blaise   You want to enjoy yourself in a villa with a rooftop pool?

Chantou   Hell is better than the sun in Ouaga.

Blaise   You want a nightclub in your house with the rooftop pool?

Chantou   I want . . .

Blaise   Shut it. You'll get your fucking nightclub, your fucking bottles of champagne, your fucking Paris, your fucking perfume, your fucking cigarettes, your fucking Brazilian waxes, your fucking four-by-four, your fucking Parisian, London, New York dresses, your fucking shoes, I'll gorge you with all these fucking material goods . . .

They exit. **Sank** *continues his writing.*

Sank   Debt is also a consequence of clashes. When they talk to us about the economic crisis, they always forget to tell us that the crisis didn't come out of nowhere. The crisis has always existed, and it will get worse every time people become more and more conscious of their rights in the face of those who exploit them.

There's a crisis today because the people refuse to accept that wealth be concentrated in the hands of a few individuals. There's a crisis because a few individuals are depositing colossal sums that would be enough to develop Africa into foreign bank accounts. There's a crisis because in the face of these known rich individuals, the people refuse to live in the ghettos and the slums. So, there's a fight and the exacerbation of that fight is making those in power anxious.

They're asking us today to be accomplices in the search for a balance. A balance in favor of those with financial power. A balance that is detrimental to our peoples. No! We can't be accomplices. No, we can't accompany those who suck the blood of our peoples and who live off the sweat of our peoples. We can't accompany them in their murderous methods . . .

No, no, and no, Mother. It isn't because our tongues are tied that we have silence in our hearts and night in our eyes. We are not oppressed, silenced, despised because our throats are being used. On the contrary. It's keeping our mouths shut that shrouds us in shame, in hunger, in barbarism, in ignorance, in individualism across our earths and our skies. Yes, Mother, I must blissfully open mine and cry out to the world that it's no longer a supposed Heaven stealing our children's smiles, our fathers' pride, our families' hopes, our mothers' hearts; but rather, an order that was thought-up, desired, and maintained by greedy fools. Mother, it is time that you understand that we are from the race of those who must die to live . . .

Mother (*interrupting him*)   Thomas, I have always asked God that it be my children who throw dirt over my old bones, not the other way around. I want my children to be standing at my funeral and feeding the thousands of people who are there. I pray to God that my children will make everyone dance the day I return to the womb of the Earth. For all the world, I don't want to have to shed a single tear over my child's dead body. That would be hell for a mother, Isidore. To have to shed a tear over her child's battered body. No. So remember this for your mother: the kernel of corn will never have rights in a henhouse. Never. Do you hear? Never. And when the sky starts raining stones, you protect your head. Protect your head, Thomas. Your head! Protect your head . . .

Sank   Mother . . .

Mother   I'm not here to discuss this with you. I came here to tell you that if I am still your mother, you owe me obedience. Blaise, your brother. I never see him anymore. Thomas, I no longer see your brother Blaise. Where is Blaise, Thomas? Why doesn't your brother Blaise come over to eat my meals anymore? Huh, Thomas, where is your brother?

Sank   He's there, Mother.

Mother   Why don't I see him anymore?

Sank   Work, he's working, we work a lot, Mother.

Mother   I want to see your brother Blaise. You're always working, working! Do you think that you bring a child into this world to work? Thomas, your share of work, I already did it when I brought you into this world through work. So, stop working and tell your brother Blaise that I called for him, that I want to talk with him, that I'm not happy that he never comes over to eat my beans and rice anymore. That from tomorrow on, I just want him to savor my dish, beans and rice while it's piping hot. I hope that my words haven't fallen on deaf ears.

Mother *exits.* **Sank** *returns to his writing.*

Sank   Yes . . .

I speak in the name of artists, poets, painters, sculptors, musicians, actors, good people, who see their art prostituted to make show business magic.

Scene Four: Conspiration

I cry out in the name of the journalists who have been reduced to silence, either by lies, or to avoid the harsh laws of unemployment.

I protest in the name of the athletes of the world over, whose muscles are exploited by political systems or the negotiators of modern slavery.

I, of course, resonate with the sick who anxiously scrutinize the horizons of a science monopolized by gun merchants.

My thoughts go out to all those affected by the destruction of nature and to the thirty million men who are going to die every year, beaten by the formidable weapon of starvation . . .

*At **Blaise**'s house, **Gilbert**, a military officer and **Blaise**'s deputy, enters.*

Gilbert   Spends his time making grand speeches while disorder eats away at the state! Blaise, this time, it's too much. Is that what revolution is? Is that what we wanted? Are we going to continue to endure a revolution that spends its time only worrying about the world outside? Is he a president for us or for the world?

Blaise   Yet I warned him . . .

Gilbert   Do you think he listens to anyone? For him, we don't exist anymore. He's the star! Everywhere, it's Sankara this, Sankara that, as if we were shit, invisible shit. I don't even know why we went to get him out of jail! Fuck! He's not even recognizable. Blaise, I'm telling you, okay: if we don't do something quickly, the revolution will get away from us.

Blaise   I'm going to talk to him . . .

Gilbert   Do you think he still has time for you? He doesn't even have time for us anymore. He writes speeches to save the world, for God's sake! This jerk spends his time playing the damn intellectual soldier. I'm telling you that we've been screwed like a bunch of pussies! Do you see how divided we've become? No one is happy. Even those brats at the Defense of the Revolution Committee that we formed get more consideration than us at the moment. Thomas no longer has time for us. "I'm going to go talk to him . . . I'm going to go talk to him . . ." You make me laugh. How many days has it been since you've seen him? Has he shown himself? He knows very well that things aren't going well between us, he knows very well that you're not happy. What is he doing? Nothing. He wants us to come and kneel to beg forgiveness from him, but I'd rather take a bullet in the skull than to debase myself before a Peul . . .

Blaise   He's not entirely a Peul. He's a Peul-Mossi.

Gilbert In any case he has Peul blood. In any case he's not a real Mossi. Are you sleeping or what? Wasn't it right in front of you that he defied and humiliated his majesty, King Tenkodogo? And what do you say to his majesty, Mogho Naaba, King of the Mossis, whose electricity and water he ordered shut off because, he said, "He's a citizen like everyone else and he doesn't pay his bills; he must be sanctioned like anyone else."

Did he listen when you told him that he had committed a grave mistake? Were you satisfied with his big readymade/recycled ideas: "In revolution, there are no privileged!"

A Peul, nothing more than a Peul, and a Peul who humiliates the Mossis. A Peul Mossi or a Mossi Peul, take him for what you want, because to say that the lamb's cord has been cut or that it was untied, it comes back to the same thing, because either way, the lamb is gone and either way someone's going to have to get off their ass to bring the lamb back . . . And I'll say even worse than a Peul: he's a western guy. Yes! He was born in Gaoua and he grew up in Bobo . . . And that's why I always saw you as the head of our revolution since the start . . .

Blaise Fine, what do you want us to actually do?

Gilbert For you to reclaim power as it should have been from the beginning. We have to stop Sankara . . .

Blaise Are you crazy? You want the people to make a meal of us?

Gilbert The people, the people. Forget the people. The people, themselves, are fed up with that damn Peul! The people are sick and tired! They can't take anymore, the people: group sport in the morning, manamana clean-up operation at noon, reforestation in the evening, laying down rails with bare hands, building schools, and dams, and bridges; no more suits, no more ties, no more nail polish, or lipstick, no more champagne, no more first-class airplane tickets . . . No, Blaise, people are sick and tired . . . They just want to get rid of him . . .

Blaise And the West? Do you think they'll support us?

Gilbert Do you want to be the President? Yes, or what the hell? Hey-oh! Have you lost your balls or what? Because I know that you're not stupid like you're pretending to be, eh! With the humiliation he served French President Mitterrand and his big mouth that brings us back to the business of debt every time it opens, the IMF and the World Bank! You're talking about a West that will give us medals and lay out the red carpet for us!

Blaise Stop, stop, Gilbert. Your plan is dangerous.

Scene Four: Conspiration 125

Gilbert What . . .

Blaise I listened to you, now listen to me: yes, he's a Peul, a guy from the west, if you prefer. No, I'm not okay with the humiliation he made the Mossis endure. Yes, he let himself tell me I didn't have the right to marry my wife because I wasn't setting a good example. No, he's not listening to me anymore, because when I asked him, over and over, to rehire your wife Fatou, after getting her fired—

Gilbert For that, he will pay one day or another—

Blaise Shut up. You know that if I decide to nail him right away, there's not a dog who can stop me? You know that, right?

Gilbert Yes.

Blaise But you know why I don't do it?

Gilbert No.

Blaise Because no one knows Thomas like me. No one. Not even his mother and father. Gilbert, you know what red sorghum is?

Gilbert Yes . . .

Blaise You know bulrush millet?

Gilbert What's with these stupid questions?

Blaise Do you know the difference between the two?

Gilbert Where are you going with this?

Blaise The stem of red sorghum grows quickly and races into the sky. But in the end, its cob forces its head down. The stem of the bulrush millet takes its time and goes slowly, not racing into the sky. But its cob remains upright forever. In life, it's better to be like the bulrush millet.

Gilbert Maybe. But we have a big destiny . . .

Blaise Gilbert, Thomas has the most dangerous weapon in the world at this moment. And no weapon, no army in the world can beat his.

Gilbert Really? What is his weapon?

Blaise Speech, the Word. The Word is Thomas's incontestable weapon.

Gilbert I don't agree with you. The Word isn't a weapon, or it only is for those who listen to it! And it's a well-known fact that talkers are never good leaders. When the Word goes too far, it ends up bringing back trouble to the one who launched it . . . Being silent as you are, I am certain that you could remain in power . . .

Blaise And Thomas, what will happen to him?

Gilbert He'll be arrested and tossed out!

Blaise I'll tell you again: his call to action can't be held by any prison.

Gilbert It's because he's alive that he speaks! You'll say, your excellence, that it's only to rectify the revolution! The revolution slipped into a fairly dangerous zone of turbulence. You had to change the crew if you didn't want the whole revolution to take a nosedive and end up crashing. No panic, your excellence. The TV and the national radio are yours. My men are ready and await only the order to release the safeties of the Kalashnikovs and automatic guns . . . I am listening, your excellence.

Sank The military, I can't forget the soldier who obeys his orders, with the finger on the trigger, he knows that the bullet that will leave carries only the message of death. I want to be by the sides of my brother soldiers who die in the wars of fratricide and suicide.

With 300 billion dollars, we could build 600,000 schools in one year, serving 400 million children; or sixty million comfortable homes for 300 million people; or 50,000 equipped hospitals with eighteen million beds; or 20,000 factories that employ over twenty million workers or irrigate 150 million hectares of land that, with adequate technical means, could nourish a billion people. Multiplying these numbers by ten, and I am sure to be disappointed with the reality, when we realize what humanity wastes every year on the military budget, so, against peace . . .

Blaise's *office.* **Pen,** *the western political consultant, enters.*

Pen We can't put this off any longer. Can we count on you?

Blaise I can't. Thomas is a brother . . . Let me handle him in my own way—

Pen In what language must I speak to you, dear Captain?

Blaise No, I can't liquidate him, and this is useless. Because if I tell you that when I ask him to retire, he will. Why kill him and have all the people at our backs when we can keep him alive but forbid him from speaking . . .?

Pen Listen to me, dear Captain: it's not up to you to teach me my job. Our plan is already well underway. The revolution is very unpopular right now. 1,500 teachers have been fired; the army is divided; the presidents of neighboring countries can't take any more humiliations from your revolution; in brief, everything is going according to plan. It only remains for us to put a stopping point to this hell, and you're telling me the story of your life, my captain. I'll tell you what's going to happen if we follow your plan: you're going to see your brother and you're going to tell him to stop and he's going to stop. He's going to speak to the people as he knows how to do, and he's going out of business. Not because you're strong, not because he loves you, not because he is an obedient brother. He's going to say yes knowing that the people whom you fear so much will put him back in business. Because he has had all this time to put the people in his pocket. When a politician already has the people in his pocket, you can't do anything else against him other than amputate his legs. Because if you satisfy yourself with destroying his pants, as you are planning right now, the people will lend him their rags so that he can sew a new pair. But if he no longer has legs, the people have to resign themselves to the idea that they no longer have a leader. So, this time, you're going to do me the honor of being absolutely clear: Are you with us or with him?

Blaise I'm convinced you're making a mistake. It's often necessary to go against fate. Maybe what you're saying works in your country. For every sky, their own sun. And for every sun, its sky. Under this sky and its sun, it's better to have our brother alive than dead. Under this sky, the dead are patient. And we should fear the patience of the dead, Mr. Pen.

Pen I don't think you understand, Blaise: with or without you, he's going to die.

Blaise I've warned you . . .

Pen Our enforcer, Ivorian President Houphouët, is sick and tired. In addition to your country, you'll govern the sub-region. The people, justice, evidence, it's our business. We're looking the other way. You have free reign . . .

Blaise I'll ask you the question in twenty, thirty years. On the ground or under it, I won't forget to ask you the question and I'll demand a clear-cut answer from you about the patience of the dead.

Yes, Mr. Pen. We're going to take the breath of my brother. But believe me, his breath will escape us. His breath will wander at the moment when the stars unite with the moon, and it will plant itself between the legs of all the women of the world, and those women's breasts will fill themselves with milk, the women will multiply my brother's breath between their thighs, the women will breastfeed millions upon millions of my brother's breaths, and one day, one day the millions of my brother's breaths that we will have killed over twenty, thirty years will flood the streets, our streets will be filled with my brother's breaths, and we will have no choice then but to run. I'll run after you, above or under the ground, I, Blaise will run after you so that you can tell me about the patience of the dead . . .

Pen   Above or underground, I will answer you, Mr. Blaise. I will wait for your report.

They exit.

Sank   We can easily recognize why the indignation of the people quickly transforms into revolt and revolution with the crumbs tossed their way in the ignominious form of aid subject to conditions that are, frankly, abject.

Mariam, *still in her nightgown, enters to appeal to* **Sank** *who is still writing.*

Mariam   Thomas! Thomas!

Sank   Watch your tone, eh! You're talking to the President of the Republic!

Mariam   I'm talking to my husband. I'm informing him that I haven't had a single night since he spends his nights at meetings, meetings, and more meetings. I've lost the scent of my husband since he spends his nights writing, writing, writing. You're one man, Thomas, one man.

Sank   Do you think I don't know that?

Sank *starts to write again.* **Mariam** *interrupts him anew.*

Mariam   Thomas, listen to me: that's enough. You have consecrated enough of your time, your love, your vigor, your good humor, your faith, your nights, your guts to this country. You've sweat enough for this land, for this world. In four years of revolution, there have been more schools built than in twenty years of independence. There are trees planted every day; dams, bridges, roads, popping up like mushrooms. This country is on the verge of being self-sufficient in food. In four years, integrity has been restored . . . So, that's enough. The country has had enough of your time. Now, it's our time, time for your family, time for your children, for your wife . . .

I want you to take the time to think about what I want to tell you, Thomas. I am your wife, and the Earth, the sky, the dead under the dirt, God, the blood that runs in my veins know that I don't doubt for a second that you have to go on, that you are right to want to go on, but without your scent on my sheets, without your hands in the creases of my skin, without your look and your smile in my heart and the eyes of your children, I swear to you that it's hard with your shadow, with your silence . . . Do you want a coffee? I understand, Thomas, I swear that I understand you and I am with you . . . I'm going to make your porridge.

Sank Go to bed!

Mariam Stop, Thomas, stop. Go to bed, let's go to bed. That doesn't mean forgetting about the revolution, it just means taking a pause, to recharge your lungs with oxygen, so that people can gain some perspective. You ask too much of the people, you have to back up to jump further, as they say, I am sure of that, I'm sure that you need a break, a vacation, we'll be good together, you'll play with your children, I'll prepare your favorite dishes, and you'll get back your strength to come back and keep going . . . Think about it, take your time to think about it . . .

Sank Do you think so?

Mariam . . . I don't know, but if the revolution has to steal your nights, your days, if the revolution has to steal your family time, it seems to me that you need to take a little break . . .

Sank You too? You're also with them–

Mariam You have no right, you are unjust, unjust, and ungrateful—

Sank Calm down, dear. You're going to wake up the children.

Mariam Do you think the children are sleeping? No one is asleep yet in this house. There's an epidemic of insomnia in this house. You have contaminated this house with your insomnia. In the middle of the night, at the start of the end of the night, the whole house, its coffee, its rice with sauce, its fried rice, the laughter of your children, the stories of your children, the bed, the sheets, your hands, the silence of this house, its fear, your bike, your guitar, this family no longer sleeps . . . And I spend all my time defending you to the children who never stop asking for you. I spend my days getting angry at the children, all because I believe in you, because I am with you, and you still doubt me? Even though I don't want to be here, I don't want the insomnia of this house—

Sank Is that right? No one here sleeps? Well, I'm glad. I'm glad my house doesn't sleep anymore. I'm satisfied that my country is no longer wasting its time snoring like a giant pig stuffed with garbage, while the imperialism, the neocolonialism, the bankers and their local servants haven't stopped bleeding it dry!

Mariam I can't anymore, Thomas, I can't anymore—

Sank Philippe, Auguste, get up! Wake up. It's the hour of the revolution!

Mariam What is going on, my love?

Sank I want to infest them with my insomnia. I want my children to watch over the revolution with me—

Mariam My love, we need to sleep—

Sank I don't want to hear that word anymore, in this house, in this country, in this world, I don't want rest anymore anywhere. Let's wake up all the children of the world, bring them to me so that I can infest them. I have discovered the real meaning of the revolution. Starting a revolution means disrupting the slumber of the entire world. Women, children, men, young, old, the sky, the earth, the animals, God, the waters, the people. Yes, that's it! To be a revolutionary, it means forbidding people to nap, to close their eyes on the misery . . . while my children awaken . . . I want to drown out the slumber of all the children of the world with billions of liters of black coffee!

Mariam You've gone completely crazy!

Sank Is it crazy that this morning you helped me clarify the revolution, my dear. Yes, I'm crazy. This country has been a victim of its elders for a long time. Africa suffers from all those learned who nap in sumptuous palaces. The world has too long been held hostage by the learned. We know the results of that, my dear: exploitation, greed, and self-interest. That is all that the wisdom got us. While fools invaded all the palaces. I want a nice, filthy fool in Abidjan, in Bamako, in Lagos, in Brazzaville, in Yaoundé, in Cotonou, at the Elysée, in Bruxelles, at the White House . . . Fools who don't give a damn about raising hell for the established order, fools who raise hell all over this damned Earth. Yes, the fool that I am is tired of your wise words. I am tired of your, "Watch out, watch out, Thomas, they're going to kill you." Do you think I'm that naïve? I'm not the blind one, here. You are with your wise words, your slumber, nay your deep comas, your prudence, your claws clinging to life . . . I, I defy death so that the reign of fools may dawn!

Mariam Lord, help me! Help me, Lord!

Sank Deliver a sermon to fight to diffuse tensions, to introduce the principles of a civilized world . . .

Mariam, *hopeless, goes back to bed, and* **Sank** *immerses himself in his papers.*

Scene Five: Rupture

Where is your brother?

I'm the guardian of my brother.

Blaise *enters.*

Sank Blaise? My brother, is that you? I am so happy to see you. Have a seat. Your wife and your little ones are already in bed . . . How is dear Chantou?

Blaise She's gone back to Abidjan . . .

Sank Again? Nothing too bad, I hope . . .

Blaise No, nothing too bad. You know women and their family problems! If it's not going home to their fathers for their sisters' weddings, it's for the baptisms or the funerals of their brothers, or else, it's because the niece of the nephew of their cousin lost the aunt of the uncle of their mother . . .

They both laugh.

Sank It's for this that our fathers rushed to weigh down our mothers as soon as the honeymoon was over. (*They both laugh.*) If they are weighed down, they won't move anymore! (*Laughs.*) So, you have to stop snoring away the nights and do your job, my captain!!! (*Laughs.*)

Blaise Careful! That's reactionary what we're talking about here, my brother!!! If my dear Mariam heard that!

Sank The poor thing! She must have waited for me in vain and now I think she's swimming in her dreams!

Blaise You trust the slumber of women, do you?

Sank It's true, right? Wait, I'm going to check . . . (*He returns.*) She's sleeping soundly.

Blaise Ah, she sleeps a lot, eh? Don't tell me that you've weighed her down again?

Sank No, Brother, do we have time for that anymore? (*Silence.*) Do you think we're moving quickly enough?

Blaise Why are you asking me that?

Sank No reason. The idea just popped into my head. Brother, be careful of Chantou's endless trips back to Abidjan! Because a jealous, reactionary, cunning father-in-law might hide in the fabric of a woman's clothes when she doesn't stop returning to her home country . . .

Blaise Is that why you brought me here, Thomas?

Sank Mom and Dad don't understand why you no longer come over for dinner. Mom never stops asking: "What did you do to Blaise that he no longer comes to eat my rice and beans?" I told them that you are too busy right now. I told them not to worry. That nothing's the matter. I told them that for you and me, it's always like between a tree and its bark. But you know Mom! She panics over nothing. She never stops saying, "You're lying to me, Thomas. I know that you're lying to me. What have you done to your brother? I warned you; I warned you both. I told you to be careful of politics. Politics breaks the tree apart from its bark. I warned you. But you are stubborn like nothing else."

So, to help her understand that politics don't stand between you and me, I promised her I'd bring you over tomorrow. And there are the kids, too, August and Philippe. They don't understand why Uncle Blaise never comes by to carry them on his back. "Papa, why didn't you come home with Uncle Blaise. We want to play hide-and-seek with Uncle Blaise." Blaise, your family is asking for you . . .

Blaise We are military, Thomas. I think you forget that.

Sank Shall I tell Mom to prepare your rice and beans?

Blaise I came here to remind you that we are first and foremost military . . .

Sank Come over tomorrow, Blaise, come and get Mom's rice and beans tomorrow. Her face will light up—and ours will, too . . .

Blaise Military, you know, right? I am military, a captain! Disarray . . . Our army is plagued by an unimaginable disarray, it conspires everywhere against the revolution and during this time, what you are doing? Eh? Mr. revolutionary president, what are you doing while all over storms rip up the roots of the trees of the revolution? You spend your time insulting other presidents, even those as old as your father, you spend your time making incendiary speeches against the whole world. While a whirlwind tries to get between the tree and its bark, like a spoiled child, all you think about is getting into a woman's clothes! I am military and a revolutionary and I will die military and a revolutionary. And a revolutionary military isn't here to brighten up the faces of our mothers. No. The army and the revolution are here to establish order in this country. Don't you get it? Order. And if you're afraid of establishing order in this army or in this country developing gangrene, I warn you, I will take over . . .

Sank Order, yes. But ours. That which brightens the face of brotherhood. That which brightens the faces of our mothers, that which looks like the people . . .

Blaise Here we go again with your blablabla, get your nose out of your speeches, get your nose out of your big theories, and you'll see that the people whom you think you're bringing together and liberating are sick of it. They're sick of you telling them how to dress, where they should sleep and with whom, they're sick of you imposing on them what they can and can't drink, they're sick of you imposing on them the pace of a wild stallion, the people are collapsing under the weight of your theories. You can't make a revolution with the people. You make a revolution for the people. You hear that? And that was the project. The project was: make a revolution for the people. We took up arms for that. So that the people can dance and enjoy themselves. For the happiness of the people. Not so that they are doubled over beneath the sun. We took power to give the power to the army because, I'll say it again, we are military . . .

Sank Thank you, brother. I understand. We are too lost. Let's take a break. What do you think?

Blaise Up to you to make your choice.

Blaise *exits.* **Sank** *is silent. Suddenly, he starts writing frenetically.*

Sank Reiterate our resolution to be active agents of peace.

Lion *enters.*

Lion My captain, my men are serious. Blaise and some men faithful to him are preparing a coup d'état. I'm asking for an order to arrest them. They are traitors.

Sank Negative. I am, myself, one of Blaise's men. More than that, I am his brother.

Lion But my captain . . . They want to kill us, kill you, they want to kill the revolution!

Sank Negative, sergeant. In any case, if Blaise has decided to kill me, no none can do anything for me anymore!

Lion Trust in me, my captain! Our men are ready—

Sank Sergeant, I don't want anyone to touch a hair on my brother's head! That's an order. An order, Sergeant, an order, is that clear? . . . Is that clear, Sergeant?

Lion Yes, sir, Captain.

Sank Listen to me: I knew that those we are fighting against were very clever. I knew that they would seek to infiltrate our family to better chip away at our revolution from the inside. You know how a worm infiltrates a fruit. And Chantou, Blaise's wife, was the first worm sent to create a rift. Using love to set up hate. That's why I was opposed to the marriage of Blaise and this girl from nowhere. In signing the marriage license, I knew that I was allowing the phantom of the revolution into the house. You can believe what you will, everyone can believe what they want of Blaise, but I know that he is just a pawn. Imperialism sees us only as pawns that it will use either against a brother, or against the Continent . . .

Lion I understand. But if Blaise is only a pawn as you say, why don't they arrest him? They're not going to kill him, just arrest him and make him understand—

Sank With Blaise or without him, they're going to kill us. What bothers them is the fact that the people have regained their confidence. The fact that the people gained confidence that there are only the people, and only the people who are the master of their destiny. And for that, we must accept to die. The revolution is more important than us. Teach Africa, its peoples, to believe in themselves, to no longer remain in the wake of the dreams of others, as Felwine Sarr put it, rehabilitate them, reconcile them with themselves . . . If we kill Blaise, they'll keep the image of us as the people who killed their brothers for power. If we kill Blaise, we kill the revolution. And that's exactly what the imperialists are looking for: a way to keep the people from believing in the revolution, by making them afraid, by provoking infighting. The hatred of people towards other peoples. If we are revolutionaries, it's not up to us to commit treason. It's up to others. The traitors live and kill the prospect of a horizon while the revolutionaries die so that the horizon can be free of all shadow. It's our choice.

Lion It's just like your story of potable water for all or champagne for a minority that exploits the people!

Sank Yes, Sergeant . . .

Lion I agree with you, alright, but for military to let themselves be killed so easily . . .

Scene Five: Rupture   135

Sank I thought you were a lion . . .

Lion No, you don't understand. Me, I'm ready to die, but will it be enough to die for things to turn out well? If things don't work with us, why would they work without us? It's easy to die, oh, yes, it's easy, like it's just over, it doesn't concern us anymore, you don't have to face reality anymore, so for me, it's not death I fear, you see? My worry is: What will happen to the revolution after we die for them to live with dignity? Won't they drown our revolution in beer, in champagne, in nightclubs, in Facebook . . .

Sank We will have done our duty.

Lion Which?

Sank That of paving the path. That of having made millions of women, youths, and exploited men understand that we are made to live with and for others and not against others. That humanity needs bridges and not walls. That humanity needs peace and not weapons. That humanity needs simplicity and not mystification.

Lion And for that, we must die, no matter what?

Sank With fists raised.

Lion Okay . . . And if they just arrested him?

Sank Choose your side, Sergeant. Are you for bridges or walls?

Lion The problem is truly when you have a wife and children—

Sank I have a wife and two children. So, answer my question: Are you with the people, yes, or no?

Lion I am with the people, my captain.

Sank Then, look out so that nothing, and I mean nothing, happens to my brother Blaise or to his men. It's not a question of courage or of fear. It's a question of politics, and the world will stop sleeping, it will understand our choice, and, as my mother says, the world will know no more eternal night. Rest, Sergeant.

Lion *exits.* **Sank** *runs towards his papers and writes even more frenetically than before.*

Sank I have run millions of kilometers. I have come to ask each of you that we combine our efforts to put an end to this morgue of people who are wrong, so that the spectacle of children dying of hunger is erased, so that ignorance disappears, so that the legitimate rebellion of the people triumphs, so that the sound of weapons ends, and so that, with a single and united will, fighting for the survival of humanity, we end by singing in chorus with the great poet Novalis . . .

Soon the stars will come back to visit the Earth from which they have been distanced during our dark times. The sun will reveal its severe specter, again becoming a star among the other stars. All the races of the world will come back together after a long separation. The old, orphaned families will find each other once again and every day will see new reunions, new embraces.

Men appear suddenly with weapons, and riddle **Sank** *with bullets. His body strains, but with a last effort, he continues.*

Then the citizens of yesteryear will come back to the Earth, in every tomb the extinguished ashes will reawaken, everywhere flames of life will burn anew. Old mansions will be rebuilt, the old times will be renewed and history will be the dream of a present with infinite expanse.

Raising a fist in the air.

Homeland or death, we will win!

He collapses.

Scene Six: The murmurs of the people

— Why does silence always need to end by adding wrinkles to brotherhood?
— Why does brotherhood always need to end as a fork in the road, obliging the brothers to take different paths?
— Why do two brothers always end up not speaking the same language?
— What devil turns the brothers away from their dreams?
— What erects walls between brothers?
— Why are there only shooting stars in the world's political skies?
— So long as this star resists the temptation to fall.
— Let's hope that it's the last shooting star.
— Let's hope that after this star, a people's people will topple the throne of the imperialist people.

Musika

Preface to *Musika*

By Odile Sankara, director of the 2018 Récréâtrales Festival production (Ouagadougou, Burkina Faso). Translated by Anna G. R. Miller.

Dreams crumble and are swept up by the wind. People are criticized, weakened. Lives disappear into thin air and dignity is ridiculed. *Musika* is a contemporary work that depicts and describes the notorious reality of the Democratic Republic of the Congo, a country whose only crime is possessing mining riches in the bowels of its lands lusted after by all types of predators.

The characters live in chaos but continue to feed their dream of a life beyond the present reality that encircles them. The dream! Yes, the dream they must constantly feed and remember the delight it promises. This is the only safe way to nourish creativity, to both leave and stay put at the same time, to transcend the real and calmly confront the future. "You must purge yourself of negativity to better dialogue with yourself and with the rest of the world," the philosopher says.

The characters of Simba and Musika cannot be open about their love given the organized chaos in which they exist. Musika desperately tries to stay in the place she sees as sacred, as blessed by her ancestors. This is where she was born, and she inherited its intrinsic values. It is also where she received all her family's blessings, including those of her grandmother, the only relative she has left, and the reason she wants to stay in this place and face the invaders, come what may. She wants to be connected to the earth that nourishes her, to recover her innate freedom. She will not yield to her fiancé Simba's demands even though his only wish is to leave this place.

I was attracted to the whole aim of *Musika*. The play embodies the concept of truth-telling theatre and brings us to the heart of contemporary dramatic writing. The reality of the present is so surreal, and theatre has an imperative to capture this. Theatre must be a subversive art as creative spaces build social connections that, in turn, feed social change. I decided to direct *Musika* for the strength and hopefulness this text and its characters inspire. Contrary to the difficult nature of the topic and the questions it raises, the characters share with us their hopes and their indictments of the world in which they exist, a place where perpetrators and victims suggest that we have the same enemy. Each person is a product of their own society.

For me, a character like Wamba (played by Nadège Ouedraogo in my 2018 production) embodies the protective mother, the woman, the mother of the earth, the mother warrior who triumphs over reality. Wamba created a geographic and mental space for herself in the margins of society. She withdrew from social life to create a world for herself in the forest. Wamba, a mother who had to watch as her four children were forced to enlist "to fight," created a new vision for herself: to be free to choose her own way of life. She symbolically asks women to stop having children so as to avoid creating supplies for the network of death squads. With this in mind, she asks the forest spirits and her ancestors to stop menstruation: "And you, without pity, hit, punch the stomachs where the blood pools. Let all the blood that clings to the guts of a woman be immediately scraped out; let all the blood that tempts to breathe in the guts of a woman run as swiftly as the Congo River. Punch and scrape. Scrape, punch." Wamba is on a spiritual journey, the only path that can lead to rebuilding our communities.

Aristide Tarnagda is a central figure in African theatre and one of the best (and most award-winning) playwrights of his generation. His writing draws on themes of urgency. It captures the fabric of society, including the place he grew up: Boulougou, Burkina Faso. It addresses critical issues and portrays fragments of the lives of the disenfranchised. Tarnagda is an author with a very sensitive soul.

I enthusiastically recommend *Musika* to anglophone directors. The play invites directorial interpretation. It is a true pleasure for an artist. It is rich, malleable. The lighthearted tone of this tragicomedy eases the audience's journey through the story. It is also quite useful in the context of teaching young actors. Staging *Musika* allows anglophone audiences to become familiar with and, perhaps, understand a certain reality of Africa.

6 Nadège Ouedraogo in *Musika*, directed by Odile Sankara in 2018 at the Récréâtrales Festival in Ouagadougou, Burkina Faso. Photo © Heather Jeanne Denyer.

Musika

Translated by Heather Jeanne Denyer

Musika tells the intimate story of a young woman who is violently separated from her love: she is thrown into a pit and he is forced to mine for the minerals that will be shipped out for use in the fabrication of electronics. The title character grapples with the realities faced by many women in African countries plundered for their resources, where families are torn apart by war. All the while, an outside narrator, Choryphaeus, enjoins the audiences to keep their cellphones on, to laugh, to enjoy the story, and, inevitably, to realize their own culpability in it. The play was nominated for the Radio France Internationale prize for Best Play in 2015. It premiered at the 2018 Récréâtrales Festival in Ouagadougou, Burkina Faso, and was performed in 2024 in Goma, in the Democratic Republic of the Congo, among other productions. The original French version (*Musika*) was published by Lansman Editeurs in 2019. The play was originally translated by Denyer for publication in *PAJ: The Performing Arts Journal*, volume 41, number 3 in September, 2019 (*PAJ* 123), pp. 103–19. There have only been a few minor revisions from that publication. It has six characters: three women, two men, and one non-specified.

    Notes on the Translation: Readers will notice references to coltan, the term *baraka*, the UN, and the AU. Coltan is a mineral like cobalt that is used in producing smartphones. The Democratic Republic of the Congo possesses eighty percent of the world's supply of coltan and its exploited mines remain in a precarious situation for those who work in them. The term *baraka* indicates a blessing in Islam that invokes a continuity and revelation of spiritual presence. General Charles de Gaulle called the United Nations "a huge, flawed, political machine" in the 1960s, referring to it as "the thing they call the UN." The African Union is referred to by the acronym "AU" in the original French edition. Punctuation and capitalization have only been changed when deemed necessary for comprehension. Additionally, the following phrases were originally written in English: "Yes, yes, yes, Ladies and Gentlemen," "There's a crisis, there's no more cash," "Don't worry, Ladies and Gentlemen," "big," "fucks," and "show."

Characters

Coryphaeus
Simba
Musika
John
Muhinda
Wamba

Scene One: Prologue

"What price did you pay to live in peace in this country?"
Bernard-Marie Koltès

Coryphaeus (*greeting the audience*)   Yes, yes, yes, ladies and gentlemen. Welcome. Take your seats. Make yourselves comfortable. Feel at ease. Don't worry about your cell phone, or the echoes of your laughter. Let yourselves go. Be transported. Transfigured. Don't stifle your laughs or the rings of your cell phones. After all, we're at the theatre, not at the morgue. Enough of these cemetery performances.

You get what I'm saying? What is this theatre where you can't even answer your phone anymore? At each performance, there's always a dude or a chick to tell you: "please turn off your damn cell phones." Come turn it off for me, jerk! As if you bought it for me!

They are so exhausting! What is theatre where you can't talk to your neighbor anymore, to say to them, for example: "Do you think that I could become friendly with that woman?" "Shit! Shit! You know, I forgot the condoms in my other pants pocket, shit." "That actor sucks; their portrayal's not very modern." "Hey, her balcony is stuffed, I could get drunk on that friggin' balcony, dancing the rhumba of Papa Wemba or Tshala Muana . . ."

Well, well, ladies and gentlemen, yes, yes, yes. Welcome to this theatre that I conceived, thought up, just to please you. I've named it Reality Theatre. Because the others who don't even want you to fart in their lousy theatre any more, those dudes are disconnected from reality. They mix up theatre and TV. Because really, it's only on TV that you can't even cough anymore. Some dude lets himself suffocate from a coughing fit, simply because he's on live TV, killing us with a shitty speech! No joke! So, I seized my courage with both hands and I went to see the sponsors. You'll meet them in a little while, and you can join me in saying a big thank you to them. Because it's the same old song: "there's a crisis, there's no more cash, *nya-nya-ni, nya-nya-na . . .*"

For that too, people, you've let yourself be screwed for years and something must be done . . . Yes, yes, yes, you've been really badly screwed! Because, holy black cow, money doesn't have wings to fly or feet to run . . .

But I'm digressing a little, no? So, I was telling you that thanks to our sponsors, whom I will ask you to applaud—I'll name them for you later, don't worry—you are entitled today. Right away, this very minute, you're going to experience for the first time in your life Reality Theatre. It's going to be magical, you'll see . . . Cross my heart. And I repeat, feel at ease! Don't let yourself get an ulcer because you held your farts in during the whole show, or suffocate from a fit of suppressed coughs. Answer your phone calls. Get the phone numbers of your neighbors, and make babies after our Reality Theatre. Take flash photos, or better yet, watch our show from your phone even if you're in the theatre . . .

Yes, yes, yes, ladies and gentlemen, you're not dreaming! So, without further ado, let's embark for magic, the sensational, the best, let's get the show started, which, I remind you, began over half a century ago . . .

Scene Two: Separation

"What can you know of exile and death when you're barely twenty-five?"

Dany Laferrière

At the edge of the forest.

Simba So, Musika, what did your grandmother say?

Musika Simba, do you really think she's at an age to run away, my grandmother?

Simba So, what do we do?

Musika I can't . . .

Simba You want to stay here then, like idiots, and let them come take us, one morning, one night, whenever they want, to find us here like idiots in the bottom of a coltan pit, or in the forest with Kalashnikovs?

Musika Stop, Simba, stop . . .

Simba What do you want? Huh? What do you want?

Musika What? You want me, like a coward, to leave my grandmother in the claws of those who will come night, day, whenever they want? You know very well that if they turn up and if there is only an old woman here, they're going to think it's bullshit, and they're going to start beating my grandmother, and tearing her clothes off, and doing who knows what, despite her age . . .

Simba If we both stay here, it's both of us that they're going to abuse. They're going to abuse you while I watch and me while you watch.

Think, Musika. Your grandmother has already lived. Us, we've barely begun . . .

Musika   No, Simba. I can't. I don't want to. No. I can't do that to my grandmother. Have you forgotten? Have you already forgotten? Have you already forgotten all the time she devoted to me when my parents ran away? Have you already forgotten that for me she braved the night in the forest to go to find saka saka and cassava and palm nuts for me? Have you forgotten her hands in the fire to treat your wounds when you showed up at our house with a rotting toe? Have you forgotten when she let herself be stripped by the men because she wanted to protect me? Have you forgotten the nights when she entertained us with her thousand and one stories? Have you already forgotten everything, Simba?

Simba   I remember well her fingers burning when she disinfected my toe that hurt like hell. I haven't forgotten at all about her joy in seeing us eat the meals she made for us. I remember her insomnia when you had malaria. My head is brimming over with these memories. But to have memories, you have to stay alive, Musika. And if we stay here, soon we won't have any memories at all . . .

Musika   Let them come! There's no question of me abandoning her to the scavengers. Let them come! I want to be here when they come. I want to be here no matter what happens. I want to be here for her last smile. I want to be here for her last look. I want to be here for her last word. I want to be here when they come. I want to wash her with my own hands, whatever happens. I want to say a last prayer for her, whatever happens. I want to make her last foufou, whatever happens. I want to bury her in the ground forever with my own hands, whatever happens. I owe her that, Simba. I owe her that.

Simba   Open your eyes, Musika! Open your eyes! We're no longer living in a land where we have the time to collect the last smile of our dying. No more time to say a last prayer for them. Even less to make their last meal or to even bury them in the ground ourselves.

We have no more time for the dead, Musika . . . Have you forgotten yourself, too? Have you forgotten that we had a dream?

Musika   I remember your very subtle hands seeking the knot of my skirt. I remember my breasts calling out their thirst for your very subtle hands. I remember the calls of the toads that drowned the fear in my heart. I remember our burst of laughter in the bottom of the pits. I remember our smells at the edge of the pits. I remember. We were going to have children. We wanted to sing. We wanted to make a family band.

We wanted to travel the world with our family of musicians. You came to the pits all the time and we laughed and we dreamed of music and of family. I remember. But tell me. What is the point of having children, if they don't even have the time to bury us? What is the point of starting a family if everyone will have to abandon each other the moment the least problem arrives? Simba, like our village, our dreams have damaged faces. They have shredded our dreams, and we have to change the dreams . . .

Simba But how do you want to change the dreams by staying in this hole lost to the world, where no one will come to heal the face of our hopes? Do you see a smile on anyone's lips here? Do you hear a word about our problems? They've forgotten us. We are the forgotten ones of the century. The ones who matter are in the capital. Here, it's life on borrowed time, waiting for the capital to send people to rob us of our dignity. You see?

Musika I'm sorry . . .

Simba In any case your grandmother is already at the end of her path. And if I were to end it for her now, here, right away, with my own hands? Begging her forgiveness? Telling her that it's because my heart refuses to stay? She will understand that I can't move without my heart. And then, right after, several quick blows of a pickaxe in the earth and order is restored?! The stubbornness of my heart pisses me off. My hands shake. My heart bleeds and makes my hands shake. In any case, they're going to stop here and they're going to finish her off as soon as my back is turned. So, heaven will understand if here, right now, while my heart persists in wanting to smile with the dead, I do that myself, and with only my heart, we will follow our dream . . . You're pissing me off, pissing me off, pissing me off . . .

Musika *kisses* **Simba** *passionately. Sounds of pleasure.* **John***, a white man, enters, points a gun at* **Simba***, and leads him away. Screams of separation.* **Musika** *sings in the screaming . . . Black men interrupt and take* **Musika***. Screams from* **Musika***'s voice.*

Scene Three: Reality Theatre

Coryphaeus Yes, yes, yes! Ladies and gentlemen. I warned you—cross my heart—that the show would be the show! Welcome to your Reality Theatre show that has only just begun. So . . . the next part. Anyway, without overstating, the largest part started over half a century ago. But don't worry: you won't miss a thing from that part.

Scene Three: Reality Theatre 149

Ladies and gentlemen, I promised you magic, you will have magic. Ladies and gentlemen, I promised you free airplane and train tickets, you are going to travel.

Yes, yes, yes. That is Reality Theatre. Reality Theatre isn't there to give you *pathos*. Reality Theatre isn't there to exhaust your eyes and ears with the umpteenth story of African children and their irresponsible parents. Reality Theatre isn't about forcing you to swallow at all costs that it was because Catholics didn't like Muslims in Central Africa that blood is flooding the streets of Bangui. Or that Kidal and Timbuktu and Gao are only tales of fanaticism—and not of gas, and petrol, and gold, and solar energy, and "democracy," and screwing them over! Or that it's because the Congo itself is a big continent full of who knows how many ethnic groups, that the Congolese forests are full of ghosts disturbing the tranquility of the bonobos.

No, no, no! We aren't here to make you swallow bullshit, ladies and gentlemen, but to calm your nerves with a little magical ballad . . . That's why, ladies and gentlemen, we have traveled the world over to bring you a cast worthy of your attention.

Ladies and gentlemen, real charity begins with oneself. That's why, here, in Reality Theatre, it's the audience who is applauded first. Applaud yourselves, ladies and gentlemen, applaud yourselves, take advantage . . . because it's possible that you will never be asked again . . .

There . . . Now applaud the actresses and actors that you have just seen . . . You're absolutely the best, dear audience. And because you're the best, ladies and gentlemen, here is some magic for you, magic like you've never seen or heard before. All this, I repeat, thanks to our fantastic sponsors who really wanted to, without boring us with details, help us with the plane tickets for the artists who make you dream tonight. Yes, ladies and gentlemen, you are lucky. God doesn't sleep. No, the guy never dozes off. And all that for whom? For what? For you, ladies and gentlemen, only for you, God never closes his eyes. He watches, he watches over our desires, he watches over our realities. He watches, he watches over our suffering, he watches over our rage, he watches over our smells, he watches over our fears, he watches over our silences, he watches over our shames, he watches over our failures, our inefficiencies, our deep sleep, our midnight thirsts, our thirsts for life, our thirsts for touch, our thirsts for song.

Don't worry, ladies and gentlemen, God watches over our needs. That's why today he sent us straight from heaven and blessed by the angels, the archangels, and all the saints ... the sponsors. And not the minor ones, ladies and gentlemen. The huge ones, the mega, the super, the international, the multinational, the transcontinental, the global, the faceless.

So, ladies and gentlemen, applaud the heaven-sent who came to offer us more than half a century ago the biggest show of all time. Applaud until your fingers hurt ... Applaud, applaud the great artists, the rare actors and actresses funded by our sponsors for whom I have the privilege, the pleasure, the *Baraka* of later revealing the full names to you. But in waiting, ladies and gentlemen, the big Reality Theatre show—conceived and thought-up by the brain of heaven itself to watch over your performance needs—the big show continues!

Scene Four: Dig!

> "For God's sake, are you not sentimental in the least? My sentimentality stretches the length of a coin."
>
> *12 Years a Slave*

John *holds a bottle of whiskey from which he drinks directly and a chicotte.* **Simba** *is next to him, his wrists tied and his body covered in sweat and blood ... Empty sacks lie in a heap nearby.*

John Well, I'm John and honestly, I'm starting to get seriously pissed off. I didn't come here to the Congo to listen to these psychos talk about their shitty lives. Seriously, if I wanted to see Africans whine, die of hunger and of terrorism and of ethnocentricity and of bullshit, seriously, I didn't need to come here to be force-fed this rubbish and to die of sun exposure. Only needed to turn on my fucking TV where every minute Africans beat each other up and kill each other, even on your birthday. That's when you say to yourself: These Africans, they're kind of funny. I mean, seriously? To believe they have nothing else to do, these Africans, than get their asses kicked, even on your birthday. And then you ask yourself: How is it that these guys beat each other up every minute, on every corner? Hey, seriously, there's something that's not right with this business of Africans who spend their time knocking each other out on TV ...

(*Addressing* **Simba**.) What do you say, pal? Good, that's enough. Because seriously, I've had my share of savageness. Yet, heaven knows that I'm classy, I am. But for a fucking long time I've just been asking you to do this: Dig! Dig, dig, dig. Dig that goddamn earth and get it over with ... Dig, dog. Dig, son of a whore. Dig ...

Scene Four: Dig! 151

Simba Listen to the sky. Listen to the river. Listen to the trees. Listen to space. Listen to the unknown. Whatever happens . . .

John Dig, dig. Just dig! Dig this fucking earth and let's be done with it. I have to fill these goddamn sacks with coltan, and quickly! I have to get the hell out of here, pal, I have to get the hell out of here with this fucking coltan, you understand?

Poetry you can continue later, but now I need your muscles, pal. I'm expected, you see, that's what the hitch is. Me too, I would love to watch TV, read, listen to poetry, but you see, I no longer have time for poetry and TV. So you're going to do me the pleasure of shutting your filthy Congolese mouth full of shit and dig this fucking earth to get it over with. Because me, I got no more time for bullshit. I have a plane, dude, you understand that? A plane's waiting for me and I have to board the plane with sacks full of coltan. That's how it is, pal, I can't do anything about it, you can't do anything about it, the roles were cast beforehand and it's not me who reserved the part of digger for you.

No, in fact, I wasn't even aware of the casting, get it, pal? Before this episode, I was the one who hired the ones who did the castings . . . Then the winds changed, pal; the winds changed and here I am on the other side, in front of you and you in front of me . . . and you have to dig.

Don't argue, it's no one's fault, it's the winds that made us change. I'm going to show you pictures, pictures of me when the winds hadn't yet left me on this side; but in the meantime, be nice, pal, and dig. You know, it won't take long; the belly of this earth is so full that in a few shovelfuls, we'll fill the sacks and get the hell out of here. You, you can keep listening to your sky and your river and your trees and your birds and your space and your unknown. And me, I'll slip away on the plane and I'll bring the sacks full of coltan to the guys waiting for me on the other side. Because, get this, me too, I'm expected. You see how fickle the wind is? Not long ago, I was the one who made people wait, but today, I'm waited for. And not for "oh, sorry, when I got there I ran into a guy nuts about poetry and I loved his voice and I really dug his bravery in refusing to dig up the earth of his ancestors . . ."

No, pal, I can't offer that to those waiting for me; they aren't waiting for words, not a "Hello," a hello, a good afternoon, a how is everything going over there?; no, they're waiting for the sacks full of coltan and that's it. And if I land in front of them with only your poetry, they're going to fuck me up, they're going to fuck up my woman. My woman, you got a woman, pal?

Simba Musika.

John Fuck! Musika? Fuck Musika . . . At just the sound of her name you squirt, pal. Musika. She must be the real deal. I get it. I get you, pal. Mine, her name is Jennifer. A real vixen. Vixen in the front, vixen in the back. And when she makes me coq au vin, fuck her coq au vin kills me . . .

Simba Why do you do that?

John Me, I'm not doing anything, pal. I told you, it's not me. It's the ones who cast the roles. Because seriously, I was classy, me, I was really classy. All my workers thought I was classy, from the first to the last. Yeah, pal, I was classy, but the wind, the wind that spins the wheel of fortune, the wind that strips us and dresses us in other clothes, too loose or too small for us, the wind that carries away your house, the wind that distances your friends, the wind that chases away your woman, the wind, pal, the wind dressed me in clothes not really my style. It's the wind's fault, or else, I'd prefer to watch Africans get beaten up, beat each other up on TV . . . It's not serious, it's funny, it's funny, all the same, to see you beaten up on TV. Even if, well, our TVs, they plaster screen upon screen with those images. All the same, you shouldn't take us for morons either. Because seriously, ever since we've been shown that you spend your time smashing each other's faces on our France 24 and our CNN and our BBC and our PBS and co., there shouldn't be a single African left on this goddamn Earth.

No seriously, you see? So, Dig, dig, dig.

Simba Apple iPhone, iPhone 1, iPhone 2, iPhone 3, iPhone 4, iPhone 4s, iPhone 5, iPhone 5s, iPhone 5c.

John iPhone shut up . . . Dig.

Simba Samsung, Samsung Galaxy, Galaxy 1, Galaxy 2, Galaxy 3, Galaxy 4.

John Galaxy fucks . . . Dig.

Simba Android.

John Dig.

Simba Polaroid.

John Dig.

Simba Nokia.

John Dig.

Simba Alcatel.

John Dig.

Simba Motorola. Sony Erickson. Tablet. PlayStation. Rocket. Airplane. Computer.

John Dig, dig, dig, scumbag. It's a matter of the roles cast. Dig, dig, dig. Millions of people are waiting for express trains and much faster and much cheaper missiles. The whole world wants to move to the moon, cause there's not an ounce of dignity left on the Earth, no dignity left anywhere. The whole world thinks only about restoring terror with new atomic bombs, drones that fly on their own to go blow up faces.

Dig, dig, dig. Millions of kids no longer know how to play without PlayStations; millions of people no longer know how to play or how to flirt or how to speak except over the phone. Dig, dig, dig. Thousands of girls are waiting for the newest models of cell phones from their boyfriends. Without high-tech cell phones, thousands of boys doubt their beauty, their manhood. Today, without a high-tech cell phone, no love. Scumbag, is that what you want? You want to provoke a love drought? When we're already parched for the little love that there is on this damned Earth; what will become of us in a full-blown drought of love?

Dig, dig, dig.

Simba *faints, falling to the ground.*

I don't have a lot of time left, I'm expected, that's how it is, just a matter of the wheel spinning, I'm telling you. Because over there, I was at home, I mounted my woman because it was her birthday.

You see, at home, we knock each other out, but in between, we think about mounting our women to find a little dignity. Because seriously, tell me where can I find a little dignity if not inside my woman? In the cold? On the streets where we're brought back to the Stone Age? In the speech that's impossible to make heard? Who in the entire world wants to be seen everywhere all the time?

No, pal, dignity hides deep inside our women. So, I was in search of dignity when they entered and said: "We're giving you another chance to get back up, to rejoin our ranks. There's a plane full of sacks that leaves for the Congo in an hour. You need to jump on board and bring us back bags full of coltan."

That's it. You see? So you have to dig . . . Please? I want to go home, I want to go back to seek a little dignity inside my woman, it's her birthday tomorrow, I can't miss her birthday. Please dig, I'll leave you a full bag if you want, even two, even three, just dig!

Dig . . .

The sun sets gently.

Scene Five: The sponsors

Coryphaeus Yes, yes, yes, ladies and gentlemen. Do you hear those screams? Those screams in the forest, those screams in the Kivu, in Goma, those screams that destroy the horizon of the Congo? Those screams of boys, of girls, of virgins with perky breasts that look like the letter "i," of the elderly, of fathers, of mothers? Do you hear those screams in the coltan of your TVs? Of your cell phones? Of your PlayStations? Of your airplanes? Of your laptops? Of your tablets?

And what is the UN doing all this time, ladies and gentlemen? Yes, the UN! This machine, as the other called it, what have they done for the fifty years they've been wandering in the Congolese forests? Huh? What has this machine done? Six million dead strewn throughout the Congolese forest! And during this time, the UN is satisfied with making declarations, calls for cease-fire, embargos here, sanctions there . . . And the blood is running, running, running into the Congo River; and the Congo empties itself of its Musikas and its Simbas, and the UN, who for fifty years has done nothing but send reinforcements . . . While the horizon of the Congo is destroyed with all the rape, the UN is satisfied in giving warnings to the M24, the Maï-Maï, and company, fuck! And the African Union, for God's sake? What are they doing, the African Union? Nothing. They organize endless summits to drink champagne and distribute our lands . . .

Excuse me, you're not here for politics, but for magic, for theatre, for Reality Theatre, offered generously.

Make some noise for the sponsors of tonight's Reality Theatre, ladies and gentlemen. If you cry out in joy tonight, if you are lucky to see, live, magnificent actors of Sotigui Kouyaté's troupe, or Amadou Achille Bourou's make us pee our pants from laughing too hard . . . If this evening, you are delighted in this show of fire, this show of blood, this show of laugh-peeing yourself from the grand circus of coltan, it's thanks to . . . it's thanks to . . .

Ladies and gentlemen, make the most noise you can for
AppleSamsungPolaroid AndroidAndCompany . . .

Scene Six: The hole

> "Don't take the path that has been carved out for us, Brother, you
> need to pave another one to the side, ours."
>
> Bernard-Marie Koltès

A deep hole where **Musika** *has found herself since her abduction.*
Muhinda *is with her. We sense that she is weak, at the end of her
suffering . . .*

Muhinda Keep singing. Don't forget that there's no night without day.
No day without night. Don't forget. Sing.

Musika Where are you going, Muhinda? Stay with me.

Muhinda I'll be there. In your lungs. In your voice, to find Simba . . .

Musika Forget Simba. He has already forgotten us. Men are like that,
you know that well. Far from sex, far from memory . . .

Muhinda You're wrong. Simba doesn't hear your screams because the
hole we're in is too deep. No voice can pierce an ear from here. That's
why no one is coming to get us out of here. There's not only the devil in
this country. Simba is an angel. Our own angel. I am going to find him
and he will get us out of here. For that I need to disappear in your voice.
Once inside your voice, you will sing, you'll sing strong and your song is
going to drive me towards Simba . . .

Musika Why? Why are you asking me that, Muhinda?

Muhinda Because you know how to sing . . .

Musika I can't do it. I don't want to think. What is the point of
thinking in a hole like this?

Muhinda It's when you're in a hole like this that you have to think,
work out a plan, an exit strategy; or else, how will you get out of there?

For centuries, we've passed our time whining while they force us every
day deeper into the deepest holes. Think about it, Musika. There's a baby
in your stomach. We need to make a choice, make a choice right now.

Musika No, I don't want to. I can't. What choice can you make from
the bottom of a hole so dark and so deep?

Muhinda The choice between touching the horizon or diving into a hole deeper and even darker, and forever. Whatever happens, there is always a choice. And that's what makes life beautiful and tolerable. Even when it kicks you into a bottomless hole, it always leaves you a choice of endings.

If our lives are ugly and trapped in bottomless holes, it's because, for centuries, we have accepted the fatality of submission and of sacrifice without daring to make our own path. That's how they hold us back, Musika, I assure you. They've succeeded in shoving it in our faces that we have no choice, that we're already condemned, that it's just like that, that it's not even worth trying for one second to stick our heads out of the holes and to open our mouths to release our rage from our guts. We are those who have to shut our eyes and follow the path that they have made for us.

Why do you think people die of hunger in this country with all these fruits, all these animals? Why do we die of thirst when the sky never stops pissing, while the river never stops running? Why do you think Satan made this country his HQ?

Musika Don't leave me, Muhinda, please, don't leave me . . .

Muhinda You're a poet, Musika. So, no tears, it's not fitting for a poet.

Musika He was right, Simba, he was right. I should have gone with him . . .

Muhinda The hole would have trapped you anyway . . .

Musika At least we would be together . . .

Muhinda They would have separated you . . . It's part of their plan to separate us . . .

Musika I don't want them to separate you from me.

Muhinda I will be there whenever you sing. I will be there, with Simba. And we will get you out of here. We will find another land. And there you will give birth. Every morning and every evening, I will bathe your baby with plants . . . Just one thing, Musika: no earth on me. I don't want their gold and their coltan to feed off my body; I don't want to find myself imprisoned in a cell phone. No earth on me. No yams or beans. No raffia. Just your voice. Only your voice. Breathe me in. Breathe me in in the morning. Breathe me in in the afternoon. Breathe me in in the evening. Breathe me in when you can't take anymore. Breathe me in until I end up in your voice. Leave me at your side and breathe me in. I want to be the catalyst of your voice. And then cry out. Cry out our suffering. Cry out our tragedy. Cry me out of this hole. Promise. Promise me that you will cry out our suffering. Promise this to me, Musika. Promise this to me . . .

Musika   . . .

Muhinda   When he comes, cry out to him our tragedy. Cry out to him our courage. When he comes, cry out to him the beauty of his father, our beauty. Cry out to him what has happened to his earth. When he comes, cry out to him so if he wants a treat, a smile, a caress from Muhinda, he only has to call out, himself, into the night, the day . . .

A star roams in the sky. **Muhinda** *has taken her place.*

Scene Seven: Musika and Wamba

A forest. Night descends softly. Bird songs. Animal calls. Between the trees, we see a girl running, running, running . . . No one is behind her.

Suddenly, the girl collapses from exhaustion. It's **Musika**.

In the dark and the bird songs and the animal calls, a face has just laid down on the dead leaves on the earth next to the body. It is the face of **Wamba**. *She lifts* **Musika** *up, brings her to her small cabin in the heart of the forest and takes care of her.*

The night descends no further; it has arrived; it is majestic . . . In the majesty of this night, we hear the voice of **Wamba** *whisper: "It's over, my daughter. It's over . . ."*

Scene Eight: The forest

> "There, unsatisfied men pine to live and die without knowing why they have suffered . . ."
>
> Rainer Maria Rilke

Bird songs. Animal cries. Dog barks. **Musika** *sleeps near the cabin.* **Wamba** *enters, carrying plants.*

Wamba   I am Wamba. Mother of four children. I understand their policies. They show up. No, they don't show up—they fall, they fall from the sky like rotten fruit and begin spreading their savagery everywhere in our village. On our faces. On our nipples. In our vaginas. You spend days, nights, months, coddling a child in the deepest part of yourself so that no harm can reach him. Then one day, he thinks he can protect himself and kicks you so that you'll eject him from the deepest part of yourself. You know that he's wrong . . . but what can you do with the baby kicking deep inside you? So you push, you push, you push. And there he is, arriving mixed with your blood, your water, your tears, sometimes your shit. There you are, cleaning him of your blood, your water, your tears, your shit, for days, nights, months, years.

There he is hanging from your nipples. He falls down, he gets up. He smiles, he laughs, he runs and throws himself in the dirt. Then he separates himself from you bit by bit, as if you had done something horrible to him. You see this tiny speck from your stomach distance himself from you. So your heart starts to bleed. It hasn't stopped bleeding when they arrive. No, they don't arrive—they fall, one morning, one night; one night, one morning, the sky dumps the sons of bitches who bark: "Your children! Your children! Give us your children to fight; your children need to fight to liberate our lands, attacked, plundered by invaders, bandits . . ."

Four times they came. Four times: "Your kid. Your kid. Give us a kid or we'll slit all your throats, you last of all . . ."

But I am Wamba. I was born in a country where there is no longer the freedom or the time to think. Yes, I was dumped into the world in a country where everything has the rhythm of the morning dew: the stars in the sky, the smiles on children's lips, maternity, paternity, weddings, the innocence of young girls, the bravery of men, caresses, the appearance and disappearance of the sun, hope . . .

Yes, I was born in a country where every morning the sky and the forest spew out more children who come to disrupt the dream of our children. Our children scream, scream, and their screams awaken our nightmares, their screams bury you deeper in the smells of the earth that you no longer recognize; that you no longer understand; and that you will loathe with all your soul from now on.

Babia. The last they took from me was named Babia. Eight years old. I had just finished cleaning the dirt off Babia's body and lathering it with shea butter. And we were eating pig's feet and cassava. Babia would cut his fingers off for pig's feet and cassava, Babia . . .

Babia's eyes jumped to mine when they arrived. Babia's eyes revealed my cowardice and my powerlessness. Blocked throat, paralyzed hands. Nothing but the questions squealing in my stomach: "What will happen to us? What is this wind that makes the innocence of our children shake so violently? Everywhere in the world children play together. Why are ours biting each other? Why? Someone is definitely fucking with us. Yes, someone is fucking with us."

But I am Wamba. I understood their policies. And I made up my mind to fight their policies. So I turn to you, wandering souls of the forest. I turn to you, mutilated bodies. I turn to you, exsanguinated bodies, bodies without prayers or graves, bodies ripped from innocence, father's body, mother's body, uncles' bodies, aunts' bodies, twins' bodies, Babia's body.

I throw myself at your feet, goddesses and gods of this sky and of this earth and of its coltan, of its diamonds, of its gold, of its magnesium, of its brass, of its zinc, of its rubber, of its ivory, stolen, violated, looted, ruined, robbed.

Fill me with strength. Fill me with strength and resilience, so that my hand doesn't tremble, so that my heart never gives in to the pleading eyes of a mother-to-be. (*Speaking to the herbs.*) And you, without pity, hit, punch the stomachs where the blood pools. Let all the blood that clings to the guts of a woman be immediately scraped out; let all the blood that tempts to breathe in the guts of a woman run as swiftly as the Congo River. Punch and scrape. Scrape, punch.

Scrape, punch . . .

Scene Nine: The abortion

> "There, unsatisfied men struggle to live and die without knowing why they have suffered."
>
> Rainer Maria Rilke

In the forest, near **Wamba**'s *cabin.* **Musika**'s *stomach has grown larger.*

Wamba   Drink, Musika. Don't make me hurt you.

Musika   What harm could equal that of losing a child?

Wamba   Four times, storms arose out of nowhere and tore away my maternity. I understand the suffering from the loss of a child more than anyone . . .

Musika   Then why do you want to tear my baby from me?

Wamba   It's a bastard . . .

Musika   It's not; it's not a bastard!

Wamba There's no bigger bastard than that rottenness that lay siege to your stomach and won't stop swelling it up. When I picked you up in the middle of the trees, the night, and the screams, you reeked of the stench of dogs.

Musika They held me in a hole, you know that . . .

Wamba The stench of the dogs mixed with the stench of the earth. On your stomach, on your lips, in your holes. So I scrubbed, scrubbed, scrubbed your body. Every corner, every recess, every one of your holes. I scrubbed, I scrubbed, especially the holes that stored the stenches of male bastards. I scrubbed, delicately scrubbed, I frantically scrubbed, I obsessively scrubbed, so that no male bastard stench lingered; 'cause those male bastard stenches are stubborn . . .

Musika In the hole. Every night. Every day. They came. Every night. Every day in the hole, and every night in the hole, they threw their stenches into my hole. And every day, every night, in their hole, I encased their stenches in my hole. And every day, every night . . .

Wamba That's why I'm telling you that it's a bastard.

Musika It's not a bastard!

Wamba How many were they?

Musika A mob. A mob confided its stench to my hole, every day, every night. A mob, as it wants. A mob, when it wants.

Wamba A mob can only give birth to a bastard. As long as I'm alive, no more bitches will give birth to dogs here . . .

Musika Simba. Simba. Simba. Simba deposited in my belly before the dogs could carry me off to their hole. Simba deposited in my belly before the paws of the dogs could rip him from my lips, from my belly, before the dogs arrived with their barking. Simba deposited inside me, deep inside me, as if he wanted to hide there, as if he never wanted to leave. Simba plunged deep inside me, and we sang, and we cried out in the depths of one another . . . and Simba suddenly disappeared, abducted by a white man. Simba! Simba. Simba . . .

I hadn't even finished hoping for him when the dogs came back to tear us apart in our turn: Muhinda, my friend, and me. I was, on one level, happy. I told myself that I would find Simba. But no. In the bottom of a hole, no Simba. Only the dogs that dig, dig, who bark down at us, and who sink their claws in our holes.

Scene Nine: The Abortion

Then the sun, the moon, and the horizon fled my memories. In the horizon of my memories, my grandma and Simba were absent. Nothing left in my head . . . which instead began one morning to spin, to spin, to spin.

Even my stomach no longer accepted anything. Even the blood that runs between our thighs every month dried up . . . I thought my belly was housing a dog. My heart pounded. I wept every day, every night. No, my god, not that, not that, my God! My belly can't be home to a dog! Oh heavens! Anything but that!

And in the empty horizon of my grandma and Simba, Muhinda said to me: "Think about it. It's not possible that it's a dog in your belly. It wasn't long ago that the dogs began to enter us. I think it's more likely Simba who never left you. Let's figure it out." And we began to work it out. Ninth day. Fourteenth day. A month. Two months. Our faces lit up. The horizon pointed to Simba in my belly. And we jumped with joy. The dogs understood nothing of our joy. And Muhinda said to me: "whatever happens, keep it."

You see? It's not a dog in my belly. It's a man in my belly. It's Simba in my belly. My man.

Wamba   Are there any men left in this land? And what's the point of a child today? Huh? To bring shame to this earth, to make corpses every day, to make sleep impossible for mothers, to be used in wars between brother and brother . . .

She lets her robe fall. Her breasts have been cut, her vagina mutilated.

Look . . . Look . . .

Musika *draws back in fear.*

I did that with my own hands. When they took my last, I understood that they needed us, women, for their plan. Yes, my dear, think about it. They are all deadbeats and cowards who spend their time in air-conditioned offices and in bars with whisky and whores; yes, these are the sons-of-bitches who don't know how to wield an ax, or even less a gun. So, they organize chaos in our villages and collect our children for their war; they make us churn out children to dig their holes for coltan, diamonds, gold; they need our bellies for that . . . you understand? They use our bellies to perpetuate their chaos. But this land, Congo, with its dead, its trees, its waters, its ghosts, its animals, its plants, its agonies, its grieving, its dances, its moons, its suns, its women, its children, is tired of this chaos, of this war. Now drink!

Musika No.

Wamba Drink!

Musika No.

Wamba Drink . . . drink! You won't be able to go anywhere. Drink . . .

Musika No.

Wamba I will always catch you. Drink . . . My dogs . . . I also have dogs. Drink or I'll call my dogs. Drink . . .

She calls her dogs. **Musika** *screams and runs. Dogs barking.* **Wamba** *screams: Drink!*

Musika I promised . . . Simba. Simba. Simba. Where are you, Simba? Simba, where are you? Dogs, dogs, dogs. A hyena. Dogs and a hyena tear me from our memories. Dogs and a hyena tear me from the memory of our tongues. Dogs and a hyena tear me from the memory of our caresses. Dogs and a hyena tear me from the memory of our laughter. Simba. Simba. Simba. Dogs and a hyena are thirsty for your semen in me. Simba. Simba. Simba. Where are you, Simba?

Scene Ten: The epilogue

Coryphaeus Ladies and gentlemen, the Congo has now turned hideous in our consciences. Now the blood of the Congolese children is in the heart of our cell phones. What to do with our houses filled with game consoles, TVs, Playstations, Samsungs, iPhones . . .? Will we learn to renounce our comforts in order to let the Congolese youth survive? How many more holes for coltan will we dig in the belly of this country already so disfigured?

Ladies and gentlemen, which wind, which god will we implore to bring back—even just the scent of Simba to the cold nights of Musika? What refuse are we ready to throw up to heal the wounds of this Congo? What music will we choose to play for Musika and her child?

. . .

In awaiting your answers, ladies and gentlemen, applaud these magnificent actresses and actors who, this evening, have made us pee from cry-laughing . . .

Afterword

By Etienne Minoungou, founder of the Récréâtrales Theatre Festival. Translated by Anna G. R. Miller.

Aristide Tarnagda, a Playwright of a People

In 2004, at the 3rd Récréâtrales Festival in Ouagadougou, Burkina Faso, the Franco-Ivorian author Koffi Kwahulé had just concluded a writing workshop he was leading. He approached me and said the following: "In my experience leading writing workshops, it is rare to witness the birth of an author. Well, let me tell you, a great author was born here. His name is Aristide Tarnagda." Indeed, the short play *Alors, tue-moi* (*So Kill Me*) that Tarnagda had just written was masterful. A very short text of ten pages or so, it would quickly come to represent the lightning speed takeoff of a talented playwright whose pen has never since run out of ink. With an extraordinary talent for writing plays and directing shows, Aristide Tarnagda has come to establish the importance of his literary presence in the milieu of professional African theatre over the course of these past two decades. His plays will never stop being published, performed, and slated for production throughout Africa, Europe, and North America. Head of the Récréâtrales Festival since 2016, he has become, without a doubt, one of the greatest talents of the African continent.

Aristide Tarnagda, Writing from Silence

Aristide Tarnagda is first and foremost a quiet person. He does not speak much; he listens and observes. He is constantly at the ready, attentive to everything, without ever giving the impression of closely examining things. His writing always starts from this place of silence and waiting.

This is a writer who carries within himself clear skies, not a cloud in sight, a sky calmly awaiting the arrival of the storm and rain. A sky that waits patiently for clouds of words and rhymes to gently form. His writing, his choice of words, they start as a peaceful rhythm and then the verbal cadence becomes faster and faster, thus creating a pressured, propulsive breath for the character. And subtly, the floodgates of words open and rains and winds stream forth in a mix of volcanic eruption, poetic breath, and political criticism. It is almost always in this way that his characters appear on stage, damaged inside and singularly focused on the urgency of speaking, their speech long since exhausted and stifled.

Aristide Tarnagda, Writing from Places

A poet is first and foremost a poet from somewhere, his locale, the place from which he speaks. And Aristide Tarnagda speaks from the top of a hill, Boulgou, from a holy altitude visible in the village where he was born.

From this altitude that dominates all that is visible and invisible, the poet becomes a spirit that can see and hear everything. He writes from Soumagou, the town in which he grew up. A landscape shaped by the seasons, that sings and scolds, a landscape peopled by the dead, the missing, and the living. A landscape where the invisible spirits of its pantheon place the profane and the sacred shoulder to shoulder, since Aristide is also and above all a poet of mystery and revelation.

Aristide also has another place he likes to write from: the street, the edge of the path, outside. The red earth of his childhood, this is the source and deepest color of his inspiration. His writing is full of dirt, colors, smells, tastes from outside. The sounds of daily life are his musical metronome ... he writes in the cadence of the outdoors. No doors, no windows, no walls, his writing extends through open doors, an outside peopled with so many things and worlds that twist and turn around him ... alone, but surrounded by all his characters who have just begun to scoop up their words with his writer's ladle; it is as if the author, like a street vendor, had opened a popular spot for all the passersby who are starved for words, for crying out, for stories. The characters in his plays are almost all at the edge of a path or at an intersection. It is from these places, suddenly appearing like lost ghosts, that they begin to speak and address us all.

Aristide Tarnagda, Writing from a Language

The language of his theatre is clear, lively, and unique. One can easily imagine, in the background of the sounds, the vibrations of his mother tongue of Bissa, a language whose chanting-like musicality evokes rap, groove, and vocal scales. This language also mixes with sounds from the street, sounds of nature and the sky, with whispers of closely-held secrets and with the violent diatribes of his protagonists. All the characters of his plays are always strangely in a trance born of the breath required of their speech and continually moving within the spaces that this breath creates.

It is perhaps because of this that Tarnagda's plays need minimal set design. The language is in and of itself a space and an extension of possibilities for all that the performance and relationships between characters create.

Aristide Tarnagda, a Writer of the People

All the characters in Aristide Tarnagda's plays (women, men, mothers, fathers, brothers, sisters, friends) are sharp, sensitive, and deeply wounded souls. They are all perpetually looking for love, friendship, companionship, and sometimes recognition. These are characters fighting with their personal demons without ever giving in to the passion of their hidden desires or power of dreams that offer them an outlook that is at once hallucinogenic and illuminating. A dogged fight against death and oblivion keeps them seated on the seesaw of life for as long as they live it before our eyes. The internal conflicts and pathetic attempts they make to cope appear to us clearly as desperate attempts for "freedom to speak, if only for now." There can be no doubt here, Aristide Tarnagda's plays are at the same time intimate, social, and also political. Each of his works is in itself a subtle political manifesto.

Aristide Tarnagda speaks for a people, his people. He speaks about the social, economic, and political conditions of his characters and, without concession, they accuse the African elites of being incapable of daring to achieve livable, habitable utopias for the majority. For that matter, is it possible to write or have the luxury of making theatre in our countries without taking a stand for the millions of people for whom the unspeakable precariousness of daily life remains truly unbearable? The poet cannot equivocate when it comes to this mission of herald, of mouthpiece for those without a voice, mouthpiece for those to whom the right to speak and the right to dream of a normal, decent life is refused.

The pen of Aristide Tarnagda is a pen drenched in acid and blood in the service of the weakest among us. A sharp but luminous pen with which he begins to cry out in a voice that is both his own and that of his people, an intensely poetic, passionate cry that serves as an act of political resistance.

Contributors

Aristide Tarnagda is a Burkinabè actor, playwright, and director who has led the Récréâtrales Festival since 2016. His plays are performed in Africa and throughout the world. In 2013, he was invited to bring his production of *Et si je les tuais tous, madame ?* to the Avignon Festival and he returned there again in 2017 with his play *Sank, ou la patience des morts*. He received the prize for Best African Literary Work in 2017 for *Red Earth* and *Façons d'aimer*. He adapted Mohamed Mbougar Sarr's novel *Fraternité* in 2021 to use in workshops for Burkinabè citizens impacted by terrorism. He is the author of over twenty plays.

Heather Jeanne Denyer, MFA and PhD, is an Associate Professor of Theatre at California State University-Fullerton and a scholar of African theatre, women, and puppetry. As a translator, she was awarded honorable mention for the Translation Prize from the American Society for Theatre Research for *Musika*. She has translated plays for the PEN World Voices and Women in Translation Festivals, and is working with students to develop a website relating in English information about French-language theatre makers from Africa: Africantheatresintranslation.net.

Anna G. R. Miller, PhD, is a translator, teacher, and scholar specializing in twentieth- and twenty-first-century literature. Her translation of the play *Roberto Zucco* is featured in *Bernard-Marie Koltès: Seven Plays* (2022), the first collection in American English of the major works by this seminal playwright of the late twentieth century. She holds degrees in French from New York University, the University of Oxford, and Vassar College. Her website is www.annagrmiller.com.

Lionelle Edoxi Gnoula began her international career as an actor when she joined the Brotherhood Theatre, a celebrated Burkinabè theatre company founded by Professor Jean-Pierre Guinganè. In 2009, she founded her own theatre company, Collective Desire, and in 2015, she established the Pan-tãabo Cultural Center in Saaba, Burkina Faso. She published an autobiography in 2014 entitled *L.E.G.S.* and her one-woman show inspired by this autobiography, *LEGS "Suite"*, won the 2019 Belgian Maeterlinck Prize.

Kiswend-sida Urbain Guiguemdé trained as an actor and dancer at the Atelier Théâtre Burkinabè in Ouagadougou, Burkina Faso. He has worked as an actor and musician in France, Italy, Germany, Belgium, and across the

African continent. Guiguemdé is currently working on a project entitled "Africa: Forms of Intercultural Collaboration and Discipline." Among other productions, he has acted in Voltaire's *Sémiramis*, Eugen Jebeleanu's *The Price of Gold*, Beatrice Fleischlin's *Radical Hope*, Eva Rottmann's *The Dead Animals*, Isabelle Stoffel's *Fifth Circle*, and Aristide Tarnagda's *Terre Rouge*. He teaches theatre in Zurich, including at the Schauspielhaus Theater.

Safourata Kaboré is a Burkinabè actor. She has performed in France, Belgium, Switzerland, and throughout West Africa. In Burkina Faso, she has appeared in productions by the Brotherhood Theatre and the Féeren Theatre. She is known for her roles in Aristide Tarnagda's plays, including the daughter in *Façons d'aimer*, a production that traveled to the Festival les Francophonies in Limoges, France, as well as to Bobo Dialassou and Ouagadougou in Burkina Faso. She played the eponymous protagonist of *Musika*, among other roles, at the Récréâtrales Festival in 2018.

Etienne Minoungou is an actor, director, playwright, and African cultural ambassador. He founded the theatre company Falinga in 2000 and, in 2002, he founded Récréâtrales. Based in Ouagadougou, Récréâtrales is one of the most important theatre festivals today. Four of his major productions have toured internationally: Dieudonné Niangouna's *M'appelle Mohamed Ali*, Aimé Césaire's *Retour au pays natal*, Sony Labou Tansi's *Si nous voulons tous vivre*, and Felwine Sarr's *Traces: Discours aux nations africaines*. He was awarded the 2020/2021 season Critic's Choice prize for Best Actor for his production of *Traces*.

Ramatou Ouédraogo is a Burkinabè actor who trained at the Atelier Théâtre Burkinabè in Ouagadougou, Burkina Faso. She has performed as an actor and a dancer in productions including Mohamed Mbougar Sarr's *Fraternité* and Aristide Tarnagda's *Les larmes du ciel d'août*, the latter of which opened in 2023 in Reims (France) and went on to tour in Morocco and Burkina Faso. She appears in a new Tarnagda play entitled *Tarnished*. She has worked at the Récréâtrales Festival since 2020.

Odile Sankara is a celebrated Burkinabè theatremaker, internationally known for her work as an actor, director, and playwright. She joined the Féeren Theatre company in 1990 and founded the theatre company Kandima. She has performed internationally, including in South America, Central and Eastern Europe, and throughout Africa. In 2024, she performed in Aristide Tarnagda's production of *La plus secrète mémoire des hommes* by Mohamed Mbougar Sarr. As a director, her work has focused in part on the challenge of centering women in African theatre. She is a founding member of the Women's Talent Association and President of the Récréâtrales Festival.

Fatou Ghislaine Sanou, PhD, is Associate Professor of African Literature at the Joseph Ki-Zerbo University in Ouagadougou, Burkina Faso. She is a member of the Laboratory of Literature, Arts, Spaces, and Societies (LLAES). Her research focuses on representations of social issues in literature through questions of migration, the suffering body, and the relationships between literature, theatre, and cinema, as well as on the evolution of literature in Burkina Faso through lenses of social criticism and the sociology of literature. In addition to her work as a professor and researcher, she is also a member of the Burkinabè Office of Authors' Rights Commission.